The
Fossil Book

by Gary and Mary Parker

Master
Books

The Fossil Book

First Printing: January 2006
Second Printing: February 2007

Printed in China.

Cover and interior design by Bryan Miller

For information write:
Master Books
P.O. Box 726
Green Forest, AR 72638

Please visit our website for other great titles:
www.masterbooks.net

ISBN-13: 978-0-89051-438-2
ISBN-10: 0-89051-438-0
Library of Congress number: 2005925568

DEDICATION

To our grandchildren: Gina, Brian, Renee;
Tyler, Samantha; Malcolm, Preston;
Roslyn, Onley, Esther Mary

Master Books
A Division of New Leaf Publishing Group

Table of Contents

INTRODUCTION:
SOLVING THE FOSSIL MYSTERY

BOOM! Shock waves from the huge explosion knock you out of bed. Racing to your window, you see the fading trails of blazing orange flames shooting through the night sky. As chief detective with the Disaster Scene Investigators (DSI), you jump into some clothes and then your car, and race toward the scene of the catastrophe.

You find twisted pieces of wreckage scattered over a swamp, pasture, and nearby woods. "Could these be parts of an exploded airplane?" you wonder. Sadly, you also find many dead bodies. Some look like deer, birds, fish, and alligators, but some are people. Were these people flying on the plane? Were at least some of the people killed on the ground by the falling debris? What about those strange piles of bones that look sort of like parts of people and animals mixed together? What are they?

If it was an airplane crash, you think to yourself, *maybe I can find the black box* (which is really bright orange). *If I can listen to the information recorded by the pilots and protected in the black box, that should help me figure out what led up to the crash, and why and how it happened.*

Would you ever want to be a detective with Disaster Scene Investigators? In a way, that's the

Creation
1) God's perfect creation

Corruption
2) Ruined by man's sin

Catastrophe
3) Destroyed by Noah's flood

CHRIST
4) Restored to life in Christ

kind of work done by paleontologists. Paleontologists study fossils — billions of dead things, buried in rock layers, laid down by water, all over the earth.

The outer layers of the earth's crust look like the scene of a horrible worldwide catastrophe. Just under the soil that supports earth's beautiful blanket of life lays a bedrock record of death and disaster, from dinosaurs to dragonflies.

If you were a fossil detective, you would want to answer questions like these: What killed all these plants, animals, and people? How do fossils form; that is, why do some things get preserved as fossils while most dead things today just rot away? Were these fossils formed mostly in one big worldwide catastrophe, or lots of smaller disasters? How old are fossils, and how do we know?

Remember the explosion investigation? The disaster detective found some piles of bones that looked like several animals and people jumbled together. Broken fossils are often found all mixed up. Fossil detectives (paleontologists) usually sort them out into different animals and people — but some claim to find ape-men and others believe they have found aliens from another planet. How can we tell who's right?

The detective investigating the explosion also hoped to find a black box, a crashworthy device that contains a recording by qualified human observers of events leading up to the disaster, a record that might be the key to understanding all the bits and pieces of scattered evidence. Is there any reliable eyewitness record of what was happening in the world before the "fossil disaster"? Could the Bible be such a record, the key to understanding fossils and what they tell us about the history of life on earth?

According to the Bible, God created a perfect world of peace and harmony, but mankind rebelled against God, and that sin brought disease, death, and the disaster called Noah's flood. God saved those on the ark to give the world a fresh start, but could the fossils be the evidence of that worldwide flood?

Most of the branches of modern science were started in the 1600s and 1700s by scientists who firmly believed in the "four Cs" of biblical history: God's perfect world (creation), ruined by man (corruption), destroyed by Noah's flood (catastrophe), to be restored to new life in Christ. But, based on the writings of Charles Lyell and Charles Darwin, a different view became popular in the 1800s, a view called evolution.

Evolution is the belief that life started by chance, and millions of years of struggle and death slowly changed a few simple living things into many complex and varied forms through stages (e.g., fish → frogs → lizards → apes → man). According to evolution, there never was a perfect world without death; there never was a worldwide flood; and struggle and death will go on for millions of years until death finally wins. If we abbreviate the Bible's account of earth's history as four Cs, we can abbreviate evolution as TCSD — time, chance, struggle, and death.

CHAPTER ONE
Fossils, Flooding, and Sedimentary Rock

Sedimentary strata

Finding fossils is fabulous fun (and a terrific career or hobby). Curious young people have probably been digging up and wondering about fossils for centuries, but scientists have been studying them for only about 200 years.

When 4C creationists and TCSD evolutionists began to debate the scientific evidence in the 1800s, paleontology (fossil study) was a young science. Creationists predicted that fossils would show complex and separate beginnings, followed by death, disease, decline, and worldwide disaster. Evolutionists predicted that layers of rock would contain only a few simple forms at the bottom and more complex and varied forms farther up, and that scientists would find the missing links required to show how one kind of life evolved into others.

Who is right — creationists or evolutionists? Before that big question can be answered, lots of little questions need answers: How did fossils form? What kinds of life are found as fossils? Where are they found?

Creationists and evolutionists usually agree on the answers to these smaller questions. Creationists can work on a "dig" side by side with evolutionists, agreeing on the little questions; then, around the campfire at night, they can discuss their different views about what these fossils tell us about the past, present, and future of life on earth.

What Is a Fossil?

Our word *fossil* comes from a word that means "something dug up." The term was originally applied to arrowheads, pottery fragments, Egyptian mummies, gems, and mineral ores. Today, however, products crafted by humans are called artifacts. The science that deals with human artifacts, and with things deliberately buried by humans, is called archaeology, not paleontology. Similarly, gems and minerals dug from the earth are studied by geologists, not paleontologists.

As paleontologists define it today, a fossil is the remains or traces of a once-living thing preserved by natural processes.

Sedimentary Rock

The vast majority of fossils are preserved in sedimentary rocks, such as chalky limestones (abbreviated ls), flaky shales (sh), or gritty sandstones (ss). Particles that settle out of air or water are called sediments. Dust on furniture and desert dunes are sediments transported (eroded) and dumped (deposited) by wind. Water is a much more powerful agent for sediment erosion and deposition. Water can break off, transport, and deposit sedimentary particles from clay size to sand, pebbles, and boulders. The same processes that erode and deposit sediment can also pick up, transport, and bury plants, animals, microbes, and people. As the sediment layers turn into sedimentary rock, at least some of the sedimentary remains of living things, especially the hard parts, can turn into fossils.

How do soft, loose sediments and the dead things, or "future fossils," buried in them turn into

Digging fossils in sandy sediment

solid rock? Does it take heat and pressure for millions of years? Absolutely not! Sedimentary rocks form the same way concrete hardens. After all, concrete is just artificial rock. A concrete company breaks big rocks into sediment size and sells them in a bag with rock cement. The buyer adds water to the sediment/cement mix until just the right amount is present to make the cement mineral crystals grow around the bigger rock particles. Too much water will cause the "rock soup" to stay soft and squishy. Too little water leaves rock powder, instead of solid rock.

Pressure may help rocks to grow by squeezing out excess water, and the right amount of heat helps cement crystals to grow, but time never made a single rock. Under the right conditions, rocks form in minutes; under the wrong conditions, even millions of years

Fossil hunting among layers of hard, white limestone (ls) and gray, crumbly shale (sh)

Petrified logs

Fossilization of wood

won't form a rock. It's the proper conditions, not time, that form rocks and fossils.

The two most important conditions for turning sediments into rocks are water and rock cement in the right amounts. The two most common rock cements are calcium carbonate and silica. Calcium carbonate ($CaCO_3$) is the lime in limestone, the "rocks" that rattle around in an old tea kettle, the acid absorber in Tums and Rolaids, and the white powder in chalk.

Silicon dioxide (SiO_2) makes up quartz crystals, gritty white sand, and glass. Silica rock cement is SiO_2 in a form that rapidly absorbs water to form hard crystals. Little packs of silica gel get packed with electronic equipment in order to absorb any harmful moisture.

Fossils and Flood Conditions

Conditions that turn sediments into sedimentary rock also help turn dead things into fossils. Flood conditions are ideal both for eroding and depositing sediments and for producing fossils. The vast majority of fossils began forming when a plant or animal was suddenly trapped under a heavy load of water-borne sediment. Scientists agree on that, although they disagree on whether it was mainly one big flood at Noah's time or lots of smaller floods millions of years apart.

If a plant or animal dies in the woods, in a lake, or along a roadside, it is quickly eaten up by scavengers or destroyed by insects, fungi, or other decomposers. Wind and water currents can scatter it, and sunlight decomposes wood and bone. Even pets buried in the backyard are turned into soil by water and bacteria. Probably none of the bison (buffalo) slaughtered in America's move west ever fossilized, and waiting millions of years won't change that. It's not the passing of time but the right conditions that form fossils, and those conditions are provided by catastrophic flooding.

When plants and animals are suddenly and deeply buried under catastrophic flood conditions, the heavy layers of mud, sand, lime, or ash protect the buried organisms by keeping scavengers away. The heavy sediment weight squeezes out excess water and encourages the growth of cement minerals that turn sediments into rock and the buried organisms into fossils. Fossilization or mineralization must begin quickly, before the embedded plants and animals decompose beyond recognition. Even then it's often only the hard parts, such as wood, bone, or shell, that are preserved as fossils.

Types of Fossils

Perhaps the most common type of fossil is a bit of wood, bone, or shell with its pore spaces filled with mineral — a permineralized fossil. The color of the fossil depends on the color of the mineral filling it and on any natural stains it absorbs. Permineralized fossils are usually much heavier than wood, bones, or shells that have not been fossilized.

The difference between a fossil and the remains of a modern (recently dead) plant or animal can often — but not always — be determined just by color and/or weight. KFC chicken bones tossed into a river, for example, may waterlog and fill with sand so they feel heavy, and they can pick up stain from the river water quickly, but they are not fossils. To tell whether a specimen

Petrified wood, cut and polished

is a true fossil or is modern, let it dry, then carefully hold a lighted match under it (a match test). A recent bone resulting from ordinary death (modern) will smell like burnt hair because much protein is still in it, but a fossil won't.

Permineralized wood has mineral in its pore spaces, but wood fibers are still there (and can sometimes be "peeled" away). Ground water oozing or percolating through permineralized wood may remove the wood and deposit mineral in its place, often mineral of a different color than the mineral filling the pores. The result (especially after polishing) can be a spectacularly beautiful piece of petrified wood (page 9), a fossil in which mineral has replaced wood but preserved the pattern in the once-living material.

"Fossilized" paper roses

Teddy bears suspended in a dripping fall of lime-rich water "fossilize" quickly.

Formation of the mineral crystals that preserve petrified and permineralized fossils can occur very rapidly. At Mother Shipton's Cave in central England, teddy bears suspended in a dripping fall of lime-rich water become thoroughly permineralized and quite hard — "fossilized" — in about three months (see photo left). Warm mineral springs can make "artificial fossils" of fence posts and paper roses in just a week or two (above). Petrified wood can be produced in the lab in about a week, not millions of years! Wood, bone, or other organic (once-living) material lying around for millions of years would rot away, of course, rather than fossilize.

Water without cementing minerals flowing through a fossil may actually remove minerals, a process called leaching. For example, a huge bone from a recently deceased elephant would normally need a person's two hands to hold it. The same bone, when leached, can be held in one hand because the heavy mineral in the bone has been leached out and only the light, spongy protein is left. Fossils exposed at the surface, or buried near the surface in sand or gravel, often have their minerals washed away and may easily crumble to dust. Such a specimen may require hardening chemicals and a plaster jacket for collection.

Because their shells are easily leached away, clams and snails are often preserved as molds or casts. Imagine a snail that has been swept up in an underwater landslide of mud or sand. As the animal dies, the weight above forces sediment into the emptying shell, and the growth of rock cement crystals hardens it in place. Since many snails and clams have shells that dissolve more easily than the rock cement, the shell dissolves away, leaving an internal mold. The size and shape of the original snail is preserved with its surface showing us how the inside of the snail looked. The cavity in the rock holding the original snail is an external mold, and it shows us whether or not the outside surface of the snail had any spines, ridges, or grooves. Even though none of the original animal is there, internal and external molds are excellent fossils that can tell us a lot about the once-living thing.

Sometimes an organism rots away completely, leaving a cavity in the hardened sediment that had buried it. Minerals in ground water oozing through the rock may crystallize in the cavity, forming a natural cast. Minerals deposited in the cavity formed by the external mold of a clam, for example, take on the size, shape, and features of the original clam shell. Some clam casts from Australia are made of a clear mineral that makes them look like beautiful glass!

Paleontologists may make artificial casts. Often using latex, they first form an external mold around the bone, tooth, shell, or other fossil they want to copy. After the mold firms up, they open it and remove the original. Then they fill the cavity with a tough substance that will take on the detailed features of the fossil. Heavy plaster was once used for casting, but lightweight plastics or fiberglass are more common now. Painted, the cast looks just like the original, and many casts of one specimen can be made and sold. That's why so many museums have skeletons of *T. rex* when only a few reasonably complete skeletons have ever been found. My wife has given the original of several special fossils to the state museum in Florida, and they have given her excellent casts in return. Thus the finder is rewarded, and the original is available for study by all paleontologists.

Flat specimens, such as fish and leaves, may be preserved as carbon films. Pressed between layers of the sediment that buried it, the organism decomposes, just leaving a "grease spot" or layer of carbon preserving the outline and some features of the once-living thing, like the fern leaves pictured below.

From a practical point of view, the most important fossils are spores, pollen, sponge spicules, and the microscopic shells of one-celled organisms and the very young stages of clams, snails, and arthropods like shrimp. These microfossils can be found in cylinders of rock brought up in drilling (well cuttings), and they can be used to map underground rock

Fern leaf impressions: carbon films (above left) and concretion pair (above)

11

layers in the search for oil, coal, earthquake fault lines, and other geological interests. (See pages 48-49.)

Special Types of Fossils

Most fossils are either shells, hard parts like bone or wood, or impressions, but under special conditions, the whole creature, soft parts and all, may be preserved.

Most famous of these special fossils are varieties of elephants, called mammoths and mastodons, preserved in ice. Partial and sometimes nearly complete remains of these specimens are strewn across Siberia and Alaska. Obviously, a rapid, colossal catastrophe is required for such preservation, perhaps related to the gigantic storms and ice sheets that built up after Noah's flood.

Smaller but even better preserved are insects trapped in tree sap that hardens to form amber. Amber can be polished as jewelry, and a magnifying glass or

Insects trapped in amber (hardened tree sap)

microscope may allow you to see veins in a fly's wings or bristles on an ant's leg! Most amber sold today is either Baltic (near the Baltic Sea) or Dominican (near the Dominican Republic).

Dendrites (pseudofossils)

You may think a mummy is an ancient Egyptian wrapped in bandages, but paleontologists use the word mummy for fossils formed when a creature dries out completely, like a piece of beef jerky or dried fruit. It's interesting that water is essential for life, yet it also breaks down dead tissue. So, extreme drying (desiccation) acts as a preservative.

Tar, basically extra thick and dirty oil, is also a preservative. Parts of saber-toothed cats, mammoths, giant vultures, and people are all preserved in the famous La Brea Tar Pits in downtown Los Angeles.

Pseudofossils are false fossils — things that look like fossils but really aren't. (Pseudo means "false.") Certain minerals (manganese dioxide, MnO_2) form crystals, called dendrites, that look like little moss plants. Dendrites in polished agate are called moss agates.

Extra cement in some parts of a sandstone can form interesting shapes that people may mistake for apples, hearts, or little "people" called loess dolls. Our son once found a chunk of sandstone that looked like an elephant or dinosaur leg bone; even in the lab we never decided whether it was a cast (a real fossil) or just a pseudofossil.

Because they tell something about the conditions of burial, preserved physical features such as ripple

Gastroliths: [sto]mach stones

marks, mud cracks, raindrop impressions, and even cylinders of fused sand (fulgarites) that show where lightning struck are interesting to paleontologists. None of these are true fossils, because they are not the remains or traces of once-living things.

Trace fossils are not remains of plant or animal parts, but show evidence of once-living things. Some trace fossils that tell something about conditions of burial are worm burrows. Escape burrows are taken as evidence that a worm was desperately trying to dig up through sediment piling up very rapidly. Tracks or footprints are trace fossils usually preserved only in cement-rich sediment that hardens rapidly. (Human footprints are unlike those of any other known creature, and have been very useful in disproving claims about human evolution.)

Many animals swallow stones, which they use to help grind up their food. These gizzard stones or stomach stones, called gastroliths, become highly polished and even look wax-coated, making them nifty fossils (shown above left).

Perhaps the neatest trace fossil of all, however, is a coprolite — fossilized animal droppings. As with the size and shape of fresh droppings, size and shape of a coprolite can help identify an animal (below).

Sloth

Shark

Dinosaur slice

Dinosaur

Turtle

Alligator

Coprolites: fossilized animal droppings

13

With a rock saw, it is even possible to cut and polish a coprolite, look at it under a microscope, and see what the animal ate.

Coprolites recently showed dinosaurs ate grass before textbooks said grass evolved.

Fossil Fuels: Coal and Oil

Coal is classified as a sedimentary rock, but it is also called a fossil fuel. Coal is a fuel because it burns, and a fossil because it is the charred remains and carbon atoms of once-living plants. Some of the stems, leaves, roots, spores, and cells are well preserved and can be identified.

Most people have been taught that coal forms slowly in swamps over millions of years. Science tells us that nothing could be further from the truth! Many plants found in coal would not grow in swamps. Compressed swamp material is a chaotic jumble of plant remains; coal comes in neatly separated layers. The roots, stems, leaves, and pollen of swamp plants tend to stay together; plants in coal are torn apart and separated into different layers — so much so that roots, stems, leaves, pollen, and seeds in coal were given separate scientific names before scientists, after many years, discovered they were really the shredded and separated remains of the same plant! There are lots of swamps and peat bogs in the world, but nowhere are they turning into coal. Scientists don't even know how they could turn into coal — unless perhaps they were suddenly buried under a heavy load of sediment in a colossal flood!

Volcanic eruption of Mount St. Helens

14

Coal stratification

Coal mining in Australia

Based on years of coal research, creationist geologist Dr. Steve Austin proposed that coal formed from huge mats of vegetation, ripped up in violent storms, torn apart by wave and current action, and deposited in layers along with other sediments. Weight of the sediments above (overburden) would squeeze out excess water, keep oxygen out, and raise the temperature of the buried plants. At a critical point, affected by clay minerals, the plants would begin to burn incompletely or char, turning into coal, similar to how we make charcoal today.

The volcanic eruption of Mount St. Helens in Washington State on May 18, 1980, provided dramatic support for Dr. Austin's theory. Nearly 1,300 feet (400 m) were blasted from the snow-covered peak, producing the largest landslide ever caught on film. The steam and ash blast ripped apart trees in the surrounding forest, separating trunks, branches, leaves, and roots. As the landslide plunged into Spirit Lake, it produced a huge wave that reached over 860 feet up the mountainside through the devastated forest. As the waters receded, they washed the broken trees, including approximately one million logs, back into Spirit Lake.

Rock fragments, ash, and waterlogged plant parts began to settle on the bottom of Spirit Lake at the base of the volcano: pollen and spores at one level, bark sheets in another, with various mineral layers — similar to the pattern seen in coal. The logs floated at first, of course, but as they became waterlogged, one end would get heavier first and the log would sink down, sometimes almost vertically through several layers, like tree trunks so often found in coal deposits. In just months, Mount St. Helens and Spirit Lake produced a coal-like sediment pattern once thought to take millions of years to form.

Many coal deposits show rapid burial over a much broader area than one lake and one mountain. The Kentucky No. 12, for example, runs from Pennsylvania to Kansas, halfway across America! It would take a storm much bigger and more awesome than the eruption of Mount St. Helens to form a coal seam that big — Noah's flood, perhaps?

Fossils that extend vertically through many layers, like the logs going through multiple coal seams, are called polystrates (*poly-*, many; *-strata*, layers). Even some evolutionists say that polystratic tree trunks imply rapid, deep burial. If the layers of coal had built up slowly over millions of years, the tops of the logs would rot away even if the bottoms were fossilized (see page 17).

Contrary to popular opinion, belief in millions of years often makes it hard to understand fossils. The scientific evidence regarding coal seems to point to a lot of water, not a lot of time, and that's true for oil deposits as well.

Bacteria form some oil, but much oil takes no time at all to form, since it started as oil! Oil is a common form of stored energy in plants, animals, microbes, and people. You've probably heard of olive oil, corn oil, cod liver oil, and other oils squeezed out of once-living things. Some oil geologists think that most of the world's oil deposits came from marine (saltwater) algae and plankton.

The trick to making the world's vast oil deposits is not forming the oil (since it started as oil); it's getting the oil trapped in huge pools underground. If plants, animals, and microbes just die in the water, on the surface of the ground, or in shallow graves, the oil gets eaten up by scavengers and decomposes, so no big pools of oil are formed. Imagine that countless numbers of plants, animals, and microbes get buried suddenly under heavy loads of sand, mud, and clay sediment during Noah's flood. The weight of water-borne sediment squeezes the oil out of the once-living things. Since oil and water don't mix, the oil rises to the top of the water, but remains trapped under the sediment layers.

The rising oil usually moves fairly easily through spaces between sand, lime, and shell particles, but a dome (upside-down bowl) of shale may trap the oil oozing up from the crushed bodies below, forming a huge underground pool of oil. The oil is under great pressure, so often when the drill pokes a hole in the oil chamber, BOOM — up comes this gusher of "black gold" or "Texas tea."

In fact, the pressure in oil wells is so great that scientists have calculated that all of the world's oil reserves would have leaked to the surface in less than 200,000 years, but there's a lot of oil left, which means the earth's crust must be no more than thousands of years old, not millions! So, oil deposits are "young" (thousands, not millions of years old), and they must have formed rapidly in a great catastrophe to get trapped underground at all. As we'll see over and over again, science makes it hard to believe in millions of years of slow evolution and easy to believe what the Bible says about a six-day creation and Noah's flood!

Now that you know how fabulous and how important fossils are, how they formed, and what types there are, let's find out where fossils are found, and why.

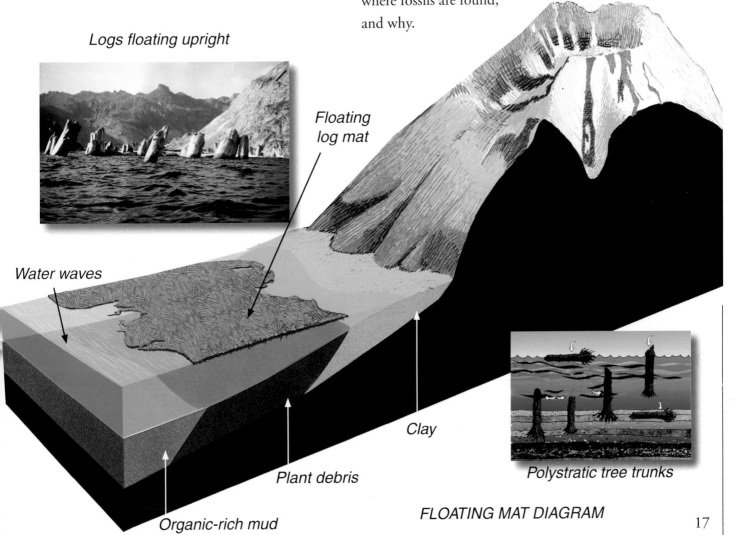

Logs floating upright

Floating log mat

Water waves

Clay

Plant debris

Organic-rich mud

Polystratic tree trunks

FLOATING MAT DIAGRAM

CHAPTER TWO
GEOLOGIC COLUMN DIAGRAM

By now you're probably excited about starting your own fossil collection, so it's time to learn where to find fossils. Most fossils are found in sedimentary (wind- and water-laid) rocks such as sandstone (ss), limestone (ls), and shale (sh). Layers of these rocks often can be seen along cliffs, cuts (roadcuts), creeks, and quarries. (Notice the four "k" sounds for fossil sites.)

Fossils are usually found together in distinctive groups. Sea creatures such as clams, snails, corals, and sponges are not usually found in the same rock as flowering plants and elephants, even though the two different groups may both be in shale rocks that look much alike. Why the difference? How can you tell whether a limestone is most likely to have dinosaur fossils or diatoms?

Based on the fossils that are usually found together, paleontologists have named 12 major geologic systems (page 20). Each geologic system is

a grouping of rock layers identified by the fossils of living things it contains, something like an ecologic system or "life zone" is recognized by the plants and animals that live in a certain envirionment (page 21). Today, for example, oak trees, squirrels, woodpeckers, and bark beetles are found in one life zone (an American forest), while grasses, lions, zebras, and tickbirds live in a different life zone (an African grassland).

It is possible that most of the fossil-bearing geologic systems reflect pre-Flood life zones which were successively buried by the rising Flood waters. The geologic system called Cambrian has lots of the heavy-shelled, bottom-dwelling sea creatures such as clams, snails, lampshells, trilobites, algae, and horseshoe crabs. It has some swimmers (the shelled squids called nautiloids) and a few fish. These creatures would likely be the first buried in the worldwide flood. A geologic system called Jurassic includes fossils of many different dinosaurs (as you suspected!), a few birds, and lots of cone-bearing plants with palm-like leaves (cycads).

Jurassic fossils may be found in limestone in one place, shale in another, and sandstone in yet a different place. A rock layer is assigned to a geologic system based on the fossils it contains, not on its mineral content or geographic location — much like life zones today are defined by the plants and animals in them, not their bedrock or geography.

It is common for textbooks, television programs, magazines, and museums to put the 12 geologic systems in a certain vertical order called the geo-logic column (next page). Given this order, the rock layers (strata) form a sequence from bottom to top called the stratigraphic series or fossil sequence. The complete geologic column is not found anywhere on earth as a sequence of rock; it's only found as a diagram, so we'll call it the geologic column diagram in this book, GCD for short. How-ever, geologic systems are often found stacked on top of one another in partial stratigraphic series as represented in the geologic column diagram (GCD). What does this vertical series mean?

The scientists in the 1600s and 1700s who began the study of geology thought fossil groups were stacked up in the order they were buried during the year of Noah's flood. According to Flood geology, the GCD and stratigraphic series show us stages in the burial of different life zones during the Flood year. The Cambrian system would be the remains of ocean bottom plants and animals first buried in the Flood; the Jurassic would be land plants and animals from a certain life zone buried a few months later as the Flood waters continued to rise over the land.

God's record of what happened in earth's his-tory, the Bible, tells us that it took 150 days (5 months) for the Flood waters to cover "all the high hills under the whole heavens" (Gen. 7:19). Scien-tists group the 12 major geologic systems into three "supersystems," the Paleozoic, Mesozoic, and Ceno-zoic. For a Flood geologist, these three groups contain the fossils buried during the early, middle, and late stages of the Flood. Re-gional catastrophes during the stormy years following the Flood probably formed many post-Flood Cenozoic deposits.

During the 1800s, belief in evolution became popular. Evolutionists gave a different meaning to the sequence of fossil groups (stratigraphic series).

Sediments from Noah's flood tended to bury sea creatures first, then lowland and upland life, although fossils of sea life are found in all layers (not shown) as the Flood finally covered the whole earth.

Creation-catastrophe model in Flood geology

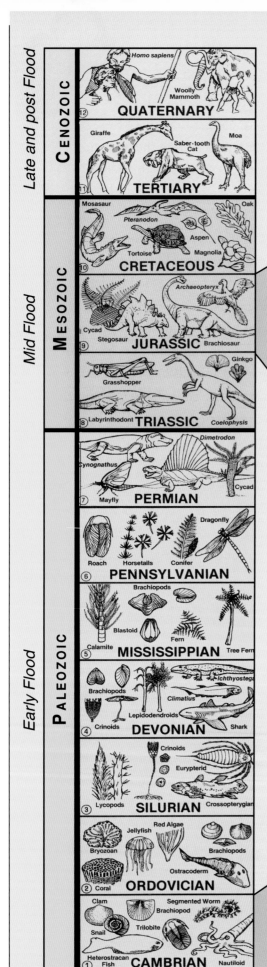

Late and post Flood

CENOZOIC

Homo sapiens
Woolly Mammoth
⑫ QUATERNARY

Giraffe
Saber-tooth Cat
Moa
⑪ TERTIARY

Mid Flood

MESOZOIC

Mosasaur
Pteranodon
Oak
Aspen
Tortoise
Magnolia
⑩ CRETACEOUS

Archaeopteryx
Cycad
Stegosaur
⑨ JURASSIC
Brachiosaur

Grasshopper
Ginkgo
⑧ Labyrinthodont TRIASSIC Coelophysis

Early Flood

PALEOZOIC

Dimetrodon
Cynognathus
Cycad
⑦ Mayfly PERMIAN

Dragonfly
Roach Horsetails Conifer
⑥ PENNSYLVANIAN

Brachiopods
Blastoid
Fern
Calamite
⑤ MISSISSIPPIAN Tree Fern

Ichthyostega
Brachiopods
Climatius
Lepidodendroids
④ Crinoids DEVONIAN Shark

Crinoids
Eurypterid
③ Lycopods SILURIAN Crossopterygian

Red Algae
Jellyfish
Bryozoan
Brachiopods
Ostracoderm
② Coral ORDOVICIAN

Clam
Segmented Worm
Brachiopod
Snail
Trilobite
① Heterostracan Fish CAMBRIAN Nautiloid

On the basis of the fossils it contains,
a rock layer or unit can be assigned to a
GEOLOGIC SYSTEM or "PALEOSYSTEM."
Twelve system names are used worldwide,
usually displayed in a certain vertical order called the
GEOLOGIC COLUMN DIAGRAM (GCD).

JURASSIC

SEA LIFE

Most early geologists
thought fossils were largely remains of plants and animals
buried in the worldwide flood at Noah's time.
Groups of fossils (geologic systems or paleosystems) would
represent plants and animals living together in certain
environments in the pre-Flood world, and
the Geologic Column Diagram (GCD) would represent stages
in the burial of pre-Flood environmental zones in the rising waters
of the year-long Flood (see previous page).
Later on, evolutionists claimed fossil systems
showed stages in evolution over millions of years,
but *science contradicted that view.*
The first abundant fossils show complex beginnings for all the major
animal groups ("Cambrian Explosion"). *Links* that show how one
kind of life changed into others are *still missing.*
Mount St. Helens, the Grand Canyon, etc. show layers stacked up by
A LOT OF WATER, NOT A LOT OF TIME.

Cambrian Explosion
Complex beginnings of all
major animal groups are
found in fossils at the base of
the geologic column.

Cambrian (1), Ordovician (2), Silurian (3),
Devonian (4), Mississippian (5), Pennsylvanian (6),
Permian (7), Triassic (8), Jurassic (9),
Cretaceous (10), Tertiary (11), Quarternary (12).

Fossils are found in geologic systems (such as the Cambrian), somewhat as living things are found in ecological zones (such as the ponds and woodlands of the hardwood forest zone). Perhaps geologic systems or paleosystems are the remains of pre-Flood ecological zones.

They now claim that geologic systems represent stages in evolution spread out over millions of years. They believe, for example, that the Cambrian geologic system is the remains of sea creatures that lived on earth about 500–550 million years ago. They also believe there were no land plants or animals during Cambrian "times," and that Jurassic land creatures evolved millions of years later from ancestors in the sea.

For evolutionists, the GCD is supposed to show a stratigraphic series of simple-to-complex evolutionary changes: a few simple life forms preserved in Cambrian rock gradually changed by struggle and death, they say, into more and more complex and varied forms, reaching flowers, furry animals (mammals), and mankind at the top of the column. The life forms in each geologic system are supposed to change into the plants and animals in the next higher system (for them, the next stage in evolution).

For Flood geologists, the GCD shows a stratigraphic series of burial primarily during Noah's flood: complex sea life preserved in Cambrian rock followed by burial of complex and varied near-shore life, then lowland, and finally upland plants, animals, and mankind. Ecology, not evolution, is the key to understanding geologic systems, which seem mostly to be the buried remains of different environmental zones in the pre-Flood world. No plants and animals changed into anything else; plants and animals in one geologic system (pre-Flood life zone) were replaced by other, already-living creatures as the next higher life zone was buried in the rising waters of the Flood.

Some sediments bury the remains of land life in one part of a geologic layer and sea life in another part. Such a layer shows which creatures were living on the land

Rock layers (strata) form a sequence from bottom to top called a stratigraphic series.

and in the sea at the same time. For example, lots of beautiful shelled squids called ammonites were living in ocean life zones offshore from the land environment including Jurassic dinosaurs. Since creatures from different environments can be fossilized in different parts of a rock layer in one geologic system, the systems are better called eco-sedimentary zones rather than ecologic, life, or environmental zones. Since they are identified by fossil content instead of geologic features, geologic systems might also be called paleontologic systems or paleosystems. Since they were buried later in Noah's flood, paleosystems with land plants and animals occur higher in the geologic column diagram than those with only sea creatures, but fossils of sea life occur in all geologic systems or eco-sedimentary zones since the Flood waters eventually covered all the land.

Scientists often use index organisms to identify an ecological zone. The red-backed salamander, for example, is only found living in a beech-maple forest. So, finding a red-backed salamander means that the number of beech, maple, oak, and hickory trees does not have to be counted and compared in order to identify the area as a beech-maple ecological zone. Similarly, paleontologists use index fossils for quick identification of a geologic system. Without counting and comparing all fossils, for example, finding certain kinds of trilobites in a rock means that the rock is Cambrian, while certain dinosaurs (not *T. rex*) and cycad plants would indicate that the rock was Jurassic. Evolutionists believe index fossils are those that lived only at certain times in the past. Flood geologists think that index fossils lived only in certain places, like ecological index specimens today.

Differences between Flood geology and evolution are so great that those differences affect the meanings of simple words like *first, last, older, younger, time, place, age, zone,* and *series.*

According to the Bible, the ancestors of all organisms, including mankind, were created on days 3, 5, and 6 of the creation week, and all lived together in peace and harmony without death. Then man's sin corrupted God's perfect world, bringing disease, death, and about 4,500–5,000 years ago, the catastrophe of Noah's flood.

Building on the biblical record of earth's history, Flood geologists use *first* to mean the "first plant or animal of a certain kind to be buried in the Flood." Scientists agree, for example, that the first fossil found buried in abundance around the world is a fantastic crab-like creature we will talk about later, the trilobite (photo at bottom left). Trilobites would have been created with the water creatures on day 5 and would have been multiplying and filling the earth over 1,500 years before the Flood came. So, the first trilobite buried and preserved as a fossil would not be the first trilobite on earth, but just the first buried in the Flood (see page 19). By contrast, evolutionists would say *first trilobite* means "first evolved," and that no such animal lived on earth before Cambrian rocks were deposited.

They would also say *last* means the "last surviving" trilobite living before the group became extinct. Flood geologists use *last* to mean "last buried" in Noah's flood, but God preserved each kind of of air-breathing, land-dwelling animal on the ark and the other kinds in the sea, so the last creature buried would not be the last of its kind. To the embarrassment of evolutionists, many creatures are found alive today that evolutionists thought became extinct millions of years ago. Such creatures, called "living fossils," will be discussed later.

Scientists generally agree that fossils on the bottom are older (buried earlier or lower) than fossils on top of them. Evolutionists believe, for example,

Trilobites are the first abundant fossils.

that Cambrian fossils are about 500 million years older than Jurassic fossils, while Flood geologists think they were buried only about five months before Jurassic fossils! Quite a difference!

Flood geologists see geologic systems as fossils of creatures living in different places at the same time, buried rapidly one after another in the rising waters of Noah's flood. Cambrian trilobites, for example, would be living in an ocean-bottom environment at the same time that Jurassic dinosaurs were living in another environmental life zone on land, with people living in yet another area, all at the same time (see page 21).

By contrast, evolutionists believe geologic systems represent creatures living at different times in the same place. They would say, for example, that certain trilobites lived 530 million years ago when the whole earth was in "Cambrian times" and had no Jurassic dinosaurs nor any people or land plants. Evolutionists were quite surprised when scientists discovered spores, pollen, and wood from land plants in Cambrian rock, since land plants were not supposed to evolve until a much later time. Flood geologists were not surprised, since they think trilobites, dinosaurs, land plants, and people all lived at the same time but in different places in the pre-Flood world. Spores and pollen can blow from one place to another, but not from one time to another!

Sometimes lots of fossils of a certain type are found together. Evolutionists like to call rocks with lots of dinosaur fossils the Dinosaur Age, for example, suggesting there was a time when dinosaurs were the most common large land animals on the whole earth. Flood geologists would call a deposit full of dinosaur fossils a dinosaur zone. This suggests there were some places (environments) in parts of the pre-Flood world where lots of dinosaurs lived. We find lots of elephant bones in elephant graveyards today, say Flood geologists, without jumping to the wrong conclusion that we live in the worldwide Age of Elephants.

As you can see, Flood geology and evolution are two very different ways of looking at the geologic column diagram and how fossil-bearing rocks are stacked up (stratigraphic series). Let's review these differences by comparing how a Flood geologist and an evolutionist answer certain questions (Table 1, opposite page). (Challenge: Cover the answers, and see if you can get them before you look!)

As can be seen from the questions and answers, fossils may be dead, but they are not a dead issue! Beliefs about what fossils are, how they formed, and where they're found affect what we think about where we came from, who we are, and where we're going! When the "brain battle" between Flood geology and evolution began about 150 years ago, the famous evolutionist Charles Darwin called fossils "perhaps the most obvious and serious objection to the theory" of evolution. Paleontologists have discovered a lot about fossils since then. As we shall see, the scientific evidence dug up in the last century makes the objection to evolutionary theory even stronger, and offers powerful support instead to 4C creation and Flood geology: creation, corruption, catastrophe, and Christ.

Questions	Flood Geologist	Evolutionist
What do you call a layer of rock identified by the group of fossils it contains?	Geologic System	Geologic System
How many major geologic systems have been named? How many "super systems"?	12; 3	12; 3
What do you call a diagram with all 12 geologic systems listed in a certain vertical order?	Geologic Column	Geologic Column
What do you call a sequence of fossil layers from lower to higher in the geologic column diagram?	Stratigraphic series	Stratigraphic series

NOTICE AGREEMENT ABOVE? YOU MAY NOTICE DISAGREEMENT BELOW!

Questions	Flood Geologist	Evolutionist
About how long did it take to form all the fossil systems in the geologic column diagram?	5 months in the Flood year	Over 500 million years
About how old are fossils in the oldest (lowest) geologic system, the Cambrian?	5000 years	500 million years
Before they got buried and fossilized, were Cambrian trilobites and Jurassic dinosaurs (and people) living on the earth at the same time?	YES!	NO!
About how much older (sooner buried) are Cambrian trilobites than Jurassic dinosaurs?	About 5 months	About 500 million years
Did the creatures found as Cambrian and Jurassic fossils live at different times or in different places?	Places	Times
Does "Cambrian" refer to the whole earth or to certain environments?	Certain environments	The whole earth
In the fossil sequence, what does "first" mean? "Last"?	First Buried; Last buried	First evolved; Last survivor
Could creatures of the same kind have been living long before or long after their first and last fossils were found?	Yes, of course	Not likely
If you found rocks full of dinosaurs, you might call it the Dinosaur ___.	Zone (Environment)	Age
Do you think the Bible's account of Noah's flood helps paleontologists understand fossils — how they formed and where they're found?	Yes!	No!
Do you think others, especially students, should hear scientific evidence that could support a view different from yours?	Yes!	No!

CHAPTER THREE
FLOOD GEOLOGY VS. EVOLUTION

According to evolutionist belief, the stratigraphic series in the geologic column diagram (GCD) shows millions of years of evolution from a few simple life forms to the many complex and varied forms of life we have today. All this progress, evolutionists believe, was caused by time, chance, struggle, and death, not by plan and purpose, and no "God" was needed.

Science tells us something quite different. First of all, the plants and animals at the bottom (Cambrian, GCD1) are not few, and they are definitely not simple! In fact, members of all the major animal groups (phyla) are found in Cambrian rock, the first or lowest system in the fossil sequence. Scientists call this sudden appearance of complex and varied life at the bottom of the geologic column diagram the "Cambrian explosion" (facing page). Life just explodes onto the fossil scene!

Frustrated by the Cambrian explosion of life, evolutionists hoped to find support for their belief in simple beginnings for life in pre-Cambrian rock buried below the Cambrian. Science proved them wrong again. What evolutionists call the oldest plant and animal fossils on earth are found in pre-Cambrian rock in Australia. The authors of this book have been able to dig up these fossils, and they support the opposite of evolution.

Digging in the Ediacara formation in the outback of South Australia, we have found the famous fossil impressions of jellyfish and segmented worms (below). Worms, such as night crawlers, are anything but simple. Each has a brain, digestive system with mouth, pharynx, esophagus, crop, gizzard, intestines, a pair of "kidneys" in most segments, and

Pre-Cambrian Ediacara fossils, Australia

five "hearts"! So, even when fossils of soft-bodied forms are found in rocks below Cambrian (pre-Cambrian), the lesson is well-designed, after kind — complex beginnings, not simple — the opposite of evolution, and strong evidence of creation.

The oldest (first- or lowest-preserved) plant fossils are also found in Australia, along its west central coast. They are called either blue-green algae or cyanobacteria. That may sound like simple pond scum or seaweed, but simple they are not! The organisms can use sunlight energy to change seawater into living cells! When it comes to capturing energy to build simple materials into life, blue-greens are more complex than we are! (After all, we couldn't grow just by drinking seawater and lying in the sun!)

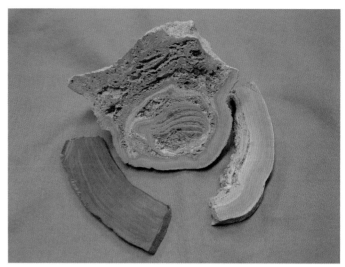

Stromatolites, called the world's "oldest" fossils, are very complex.

CAMBRIAN EXPLOSION —
Sudden appearance of all major animal groups at base of geologic column.

(1) Crinoids, (2) Jellyfish, (3) Sponges, (4) Starfish, (5) Trilobites, (6) Nautiloids, (7) Clam, (8) Brachiopods, (9) Sea Urchins, (10) Segmented worm, (11) Snail, (12) Coral

Rafting in the Grand Canyon

There's more. Blue-greens grow as mossy mats on rocks in the tidal zone along the shore. The mats trap and then cement sand grains to form a mineral layer, continually building new layers on top of earlier ones. The banded rock deposits they produce are called stromatolites. Right off the west coast of Australia where the world's oldest (first-preserved) fossils are found, living blue-greens are still producing stromatolites. What's the lesson? Evolution? No! Creation? Yes! It's complex beginnings, evidence that living things were created well designed to multiply after their kinds.

A Lot of Water, Not a Lot of Time: The Grand Canyon

Some evolutionists admit that fossils suggest complex beginnings and multiplication after kind, but they still want people to believe it took millions of years to stack up rocks in layers like we see at the Grand Canyon. Arizona's awesome canyon averages about one mile (1.6 km) deep and ten miles (16 km) wide, and it traps the Colorado River for over 250 miles (400 km). Before I became a Christian and a scientist trained in fossil study, I thought people who looked at the Grand Canyon would see the proof of evolution and just throw their Bibles over the edge. Now I've led over 40 week-long

hikes and two raft trips through the canyon, and I'm ready to stake the place out with Bible verses!

At the base of the canyon, most strikingly visible to river rafters, are what could be called creation and pre-Flood rocks. The crystalline granites and schists may be the remnants of the continental crust God created and raised above the waters on day 3 (Gen. 1:9–10). On top of this

Crystalline basement rock

28

created "crystalline basement" are various types and amounts of pre-Flood sedimentary rocks. These sediments may have been deposited from rivers, lakes, and seas during the nearly 1,600 years between the Fall and the Flood. Because they were laid down slowly, a little at a time, these pre-Flood rocks contain hardly any fossils and they only form "clumps" here and there.

If evolution were true, all sedimentary deposits would be found in small areas with few or no fossils. It really takes catastrophic, continent-covering flooding such as Noah's flood to produce vast horizontal sheets of fossil-rich layers; and that is what is found piled on top of the pre-Flood rocks at the Grand Canyon. Running underground, these layers of Flood rock stretch for thousands of square miles across much of North America!

According to the Bible, the Flood began when "all the fountains of the great deep" burst forth (Gen. 7:11). About two-thirds of what comes out of the average volcano is water vapor. That super-heated, extremely pressurized water in molten underground rock (magma) seems to be the major source of both the water and the power of Noah's flood. The volcanic eruption that blew the top off Mount St. Helens released the energy of 20,000 atomic bombs, but that was nothing compared to scores of much larger volcanoes whose eruptions may have split the continents at the beginning of the Flood.

When the "fountains of the great deep" burst forth where the Grand Canyon is now, the force tilted the creation and pre-Flood rocks out of the way. Some of the tilted pre-Flood rocks were soft and crumbly (like the Hakatai Shale); some were very hard (especially the Shinumo Quartzite). When Noah's flood washed a slurry of sand into the area (the future Tapeats Sandstone), the current was so fast and furious that it sheared off the tilted layers of hard and soft rock in a nearly straight line. If evolution were true and the erosion occurred gradually over millions of years, the softer rock would be gone and the hard rock would stick up into the sediment above.

The Flood was so powerful, however, that the hard and soft rock layers were cut off almost equally. Only the extremely hard Shinumo rock offered some resistance to the Flood current — but the Tapeats current broke off huge boulders of that very hard rock (up to 30 feet or 9 m in diameter!) and carried them downstream for miles (page 31)! By contrast, today's "mighty" Colorado River can barely move much smaller boulders from the mouths of side canyons. Something MUCH more awesome than the Colorado River moved these huge, hard boulders.

As the Flood continued to wash sediments into the future Grand Canyon area, it "forgot about" evolution and millions of years. At the contact

1 Kaibab Limestone
2 Toroweap Formation
3 Coconino Sandstone
4 Hermit Shale
5 Supai Formation
6 Redwall Limestone
7 Muav Limestone
8 Bright Angel Shale
9 Tapeats Sandstone

between Redwall and Muav Limestones, the Flood deposited fossils from GCD5 (Mississippian) directly on top of fossils from GCD1 (Cambrian). For those who believe in "evolutionary time," that means 150 million "evolutionary years" are missing. Evolutionists believe life preserved in GCD1 must evolve into the life preserved in the three missing systems (GCD 2, 3, 4) before it can evolve into GCD5 life. Skipping 150 million years of evolutionary time would break the evolutionary chain and make evolution impossible. So evolutionists went looking for evidence of erosion, and they were honest enough to admit they did not find it. They did find a little erosion here and there, but no evidence of anything that could erase the rock they thought took 150 million years to form.

Fossil systems high in the GCD are often found directly on top of systems much lower with gaps of millions of evolutionary years. If there is no evidence of sufficient erosion between the "out of place" systems, their contact line is called a paraconformity and evolutionists rightly treat these as major mysteries. For Flood geologists there is no mystery at all. Instead, paraconformities are direct and scientific evidence that the evolutionists' millions of years are

a myth. Flood geologists treat geologic systems as the fossilized remains of plants and animals living in different places at the same time in the pre-Flood world. So a paraconformity just means one environment was directly deposited on top of another with little or no erosion and no missing time — just as the evidence shows! Once again, belief in a lot of time makes it hard to understand the scientific evidence; belief in a lot of water makes it easy!

What about the Coconino Sandstone? That layer, now seen as a bright white cliff not far below the canyon rim, is cross-bedded like the sand in a desert dune. Evolutionists once called this a desert deposit that disproved Flood geology. However, dunes also form and travel underwater; ripple marks in the sand just offshore are mini-dunes, and big dunes can be found 60 feet (20 m) under the ocean's surface. The roundness of the sand grains, steepness of the cross-beds, and preserved animal trackways all suggest scientifically that the Coconino was formed underwater, not in a desert

— further confirming, not contradicting, Flood geology.

By the middle of Noah's flood, however, all the layers now seen at the Grand Canyon were underwater, and there was no canyon. How did these layers end up nearly 9,000 feet (2,800 m) above sea level, and what formed the big gash (the Grand Canyon), now cut a mile (1.6 km) into these layers?

At the end of the Flood, it seems God repeated what He did on day 3 when He caused the dry land to rise from a world covered with water: "The mountains rose

Huge boulders like those in the Tapeats Sandstone

and the valleys sank down" (Ps. 104:8). This time, the "mountains rose" covered with layers of Flood sediment that soon hardened into sedimentary rock. The receding Flood waters drained into the new ocean basins as the "valleys sank." In places, however, the rising land trapped some of the floodwaters behind natural earthen dams. The area now called the Grand Canyon was at first a "Grand Dam," the Kaibab

Upwarp, that trapped huge amounts of water in three huge lakes (as large as three Great Lakes) in what we now call northern Arizona and southern Utah.

During the icy, stormy conditions that prevailed for decades and centuries after Noah left the ark, snow melt and rainwater continued to pile up water behind the Grand Dam. Then the dam broke. Flowing rapidly downhill from nearly 9,000 feet (2,800 m), the surging waters soon reached speeds at which they formed special bubbles called cavitations. When they hit surfaces, cavitation bubbles implode, producing shock waves that pulverize rock like hand grenades would. When water was released too fast through a bypass tunnel at the base of the man-made Glen Canyon Dam, cavitation bubbles ate through the steel-reinforced concrete tubes in less than one minute. Cavitation bubbles forming and imploding on a grand scale would pulverize the natural post-Flood Grand Dam very

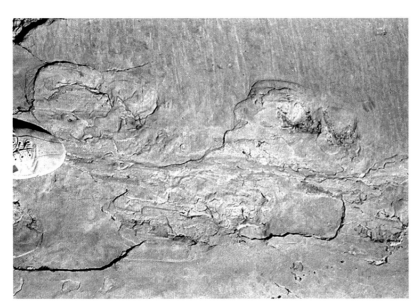

Animal trackway in Coconino sandstone

quickly indeed. In perhaps only weeks or months, drainage of the three impounded lakes through the rapidly widening and deepening breach in the Grand Dam would leave behind the Grand Canyon with the tiny trickle called the Colorado River trapped in its inner gorge.

The breached dam concept for the rapid formation of the Grand Canyon was first proposed by creationists/Flood geologists such as Dr. Steve Austin at the Institute for Creation Research (ICR). It fits the evidence so well that some evolutionists now accept the idea.

Dramatic support for the view was provided by the second modern eruption of Mount St. Helens in June 1982. A monumental mud flow cut down through multiple layers of rock, cutting a zigzag main canyon with amphitheater-head side canyons, forming a 1:40 scale model of the Grand Canyon in just five days, complete with a little stream left behind in the canyon bottom!

You can imagine one day when the trees grow back, that an evolutionist wanders into the "little grand canyon" on the flanks of Mount St. Helens and begins to wonder how many millions of years it took that little stream to form that big canyon. But the stream didn't cut the canyon. As it was at the Grand Canyon, the canyon came first; the river came second — trapped in a huge canyon formed by a lot of water, not a lot of time.

Sometimes I like to think about a paleontologist who has spent 20 years studying the Grand Canyon. Finally he takes a break, walks up to the rim, and sits on a bench. There's a Gideon Bible. As he begins to read the Bible, he begins to shout with excitement: (1) "Now I know why every time I find a fossil here in the Grand Canyon it seems so marvelously well designed. Life is not a product of time and chance; life is a gift of God, created with plan and purpose!" (2) "Now I know why the canyon walls are full of fossilized dead things. Man's sin and rebellion against God brought struggle and death into the

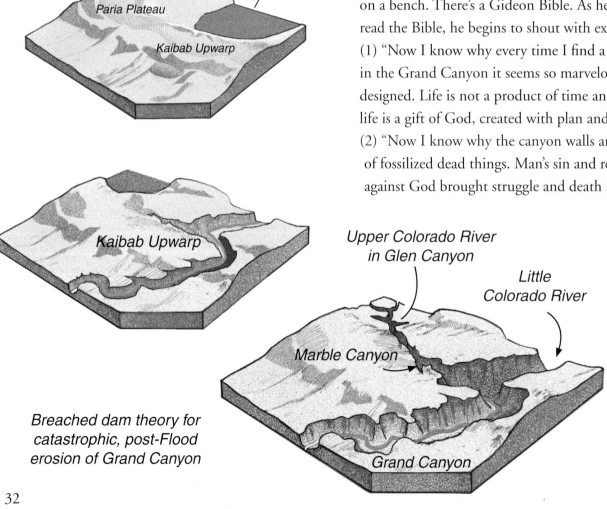

Canyonlands Lake
(southwest corner)

Hopi Lake
(northwest corner)

Paria Plateau

Kaibab Upwarp

Kaibab Upwarp

Upper Colorado River
in Glen Canyon

Little
Colorado River

Marble Canyon

Breached dam theory for catastrophic, post-Flood erosion of Grand Canyon

Grand Canyon

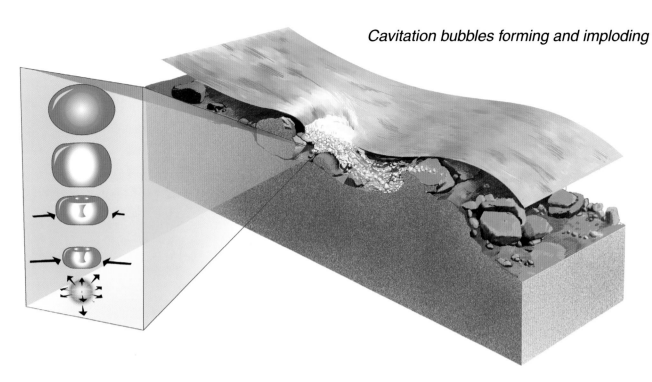

Cavitation bubbles forming and imploding

world God had created 'all very good.'" (3) "Now I know how billions of dead things got buried in rock layers stacked up over a mile deep. Now I know how the hard and soft layers in the inner gorge got tilted up and sheared off, how those big boulders got moved, and how this little river got trapped in such a huge canyon. Now I know how you can skip millions of mythical years with no evidence for erosion. It was a lot of water, not a lot of time, that stacked up these layers and cut this awesome canyon, the waters of Noah's flood." (4) "Here I am looking at it. The Flood would have destroyed all land life on earth, but God provided the ark as a way of escape to safety. God can conquer death for me, too, and give me new life in Jesus Christ!"

Wow! The good news of the gospel can be seen even in the fossils and rock at the Grand Canyon. It's a site worthy of visiting at least once in a lifetime.

Grand MISSIONARY Canyon

1) Creation
The lowest fossil-rich layer (Cambrian)
contains complex and varied life, well designed
to multiply after kind.

2) Corruption
The layers of fossils show death, disease, disaster, and
decline — a result of man's sin.

3) Catastrophe
Vast, fast processes (like those in Noah's flood) were required
to tilt and shear pre-Cambrian rocks and to skip "150 million
mythical years" without erosion.

4) Christ
Raised above the sea, the beauty of the canyon points to
restoration and new life in Christ.

33

CHAPTER FOUR
KINDS OF FOSSILS I: INVERTEBRATES

Nautilus

Are you ready to dig up some fossils? This chapter will help you identify what you find. It will also help you see why fossils have been such an encouragement to creationists, and such a disappointment to evolutionists. Over 95 percent of all fossils found are seashells, so let's start our look at fossil kinds with the remains of creatures that wrap their bodies in a hard shell that makes them easy to preserve. Because they have no backbones, these creatures are called invertebrates.

Mollusks

Mollusks

Clams, snails, and the squid-octopus group belong to a large category (phylum) of animals called mollusks. Their name means "soft-bodied," but that only means there are no bones in their meat. They have a thick, muscular body with lots of complex organs inside: a nervous system with a brain (sometimes three!) and sense organs for smell and often for sight (eyes); a complete digestive system with many organs; and systems for circulation (arteries, veins, and one or more hearts), excretion (kidneys), and respiration (gills for breathing underwater or on land).

Among the most complex of all the invertebrates are the squid and octopus in the mollusk class called cephalopods, which means "head-footed," since their tentacles come out of their heads. The octopus is smart enough to learn its way through mazes and to escape captivity. The giant squid, over 75 feet (23 m) long, uses its powerful "parrot beak" jaws and its tentacles full of suction cups to attack, kill, and eat whales (while some whales, in turn, eat young squids)! The giant squid can jet propel itself out of the water, trailing the long, wriggling tentacles that are no doubt responsible for some wild sea serpent stories!

The squid's eye is the world's biggest at ten inches (25 cm) across. The eye of a cephalopod looks and works like ours. That's another mystery for evolution. Evolutionists want to believe that organs built on the same plan (homology) show evolution from a common ancestor that first had that plan, but the assumed common ancestor of a squid and human being was

Side by side comparison of modern-day and fossilized snails

supposed to be some kind of worm that had no eye like that at all! Evolutionists like to call that convergence, meaning two organs look alike even though they did *not* come from a common ancestor with that organ — the opposite of evolution. Creationists see the cephalopod eye and the human eye as another example of creation according to a common plan, in this case a plan that seems designed to make sure we don't fall for evolution!

Most mollusks wrap up their bodies in a thick shell of calcium carbonate ($CaCO_3$). Mollusk shells come in a dazzling array of shapes

Snail shells

and colors, showing us that God is not only the greatest scientist, but the greatest artist as well! A branch of science (malacology) is devoted to the study of mollusk shells, and many are highly prized as art objects.

It's the mollusk shell, or its impression, that is usually found as a fossil. The form of calcium carbonate usually found in mollusk shells (aragonite) dissolves more easily than calcite, so many mollusk fossils are found as internal and external molds and casts. They show us the shape and inside or outside surface of the shell, even though most or all of the shell is gone.

Snails belong to the mollusk class called gastropods (which means "stomach-footed," since they walk on their stomachs). Snails today can be high- or low-spired, with or without spines, having large or small openings, and just about any number of other variables — and fossil snails show the same features. Snail fossils from the first-buried (Cambrian) right up through the stratigraphic sequence seem to show that snails were created well designed to multiply after their kinds, with lots of variation in form and beauty. Evolutionists don't even try to tell us what animal evolved into snails, or which snail was the ancestor of others. The comparison above shows modern and fossil snails side by side; no evolution there!

Beauty of form and color in mollusks (Gen. 2:9)

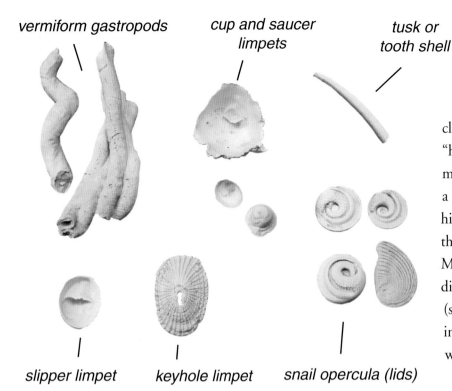

vermiform gastropods

cup and saucer limpets

tusk or tooth shell

slipper limpet

keyhole limpet

snail opercula (lids)

Clams belong to the mollusk class called pelecypods, which means "hatchet-footed." Clams are bivalves, meaning they have two shells joined at a hinge. When their muscles relax, the hinge springs the two shells open, and the hatchet-shaped foot can come out. Many clams use the hatchet foot to dig deeply into sand, extending tubes (siphons) up into the water for filtering food. Some can even bore into wood or rock.

When a clam dies, the muscle relaxes and the shell opens. When the hinge rots, the two halves separate.

Above are members of the gastropod class different from the "usual" snail. Those with low or no twist that give them the shape of a kneecap (patella) are called patelliform gastropods. Included are the beautiful (and delicious) abalones and the limpets, which come in slipper, cup-and-saucer, and keyhole or volcano shapes. Vermiform (worm-shaped) gastropods start as ordinary snails, but then form loose, open coils that look like worm tubes. A scaphapod is a small, hollow, curved shell called a tusk or tooth shell.

Many snails have lids (opercula) that can be used to close the opening when the snail pulls back into its shell. Most opercula are shaped like little pennies, and some have neat designs like those called cat's eyes. Sometimes the lids are found in one layer of a fossil deposit and the rest of the shell is found in a different layer. Obviously, they did not evolve in different time zones! That pattern shows that the action of flowing water separates things into different layers according to shape and density — a lot of water again, not a lot of time.

Unless they've just recently died, most of the clams you'll find on a beach will be separate halves, but many fossil clams are found complete, with both halves still together. That means the clam must have been buried so deeply and so fast that it couldn't even open its shell to burrow out — and many clams can dig through many feet (a few meters) of sand! Closed clams testify to rapid, deep burial, sometimes on a grand scale — perhaps yet another reminder of Noah's flood.

Clams can also provide evidence that evolution's millions of years are a myth. In a shell pit near our home in Florida, we found a clam fossil believed by evolutionists to be

Clam shells

an index for a time 2–5 million years ago, but there was still flesh on the hinge that had not rotted! An expert confirmed that Mary had correctly identified the index clam, and admitted that this — and many other specimens he knew about — posed a serious problem for belief in millions of years!

A fantastic variety of fossil clams looking very much like those we have today is scattered abundantly throughout the geologic column, so it appears that clams, like snails, were designed to multiply after kind. In the first half of the 1900s, evolutionists claimed they had a series of fossils that showed how flat oysters evolved into coiled oysters over millions of years. Sure enough, in sedimentary layers off England, flat oysters were found on the bottom, slightly coiled ones farther up, finally reaching a super-coiled form that became extinct, the evolutionary story went, when one shell coiled over the other and pinned it shut so the coiled oyster could no longer feed. Like so many evolutionary stories, it seemed like a good story until more evidence was discovered. When he flicked a bit of mud out of the way, a student discovered the coiled oyster had not pinned itself shut after all.

Then, off Greenland, fossil oysters were found in reverse order, coiled in bottom layers and flat on top. Finally, paleontologists noticed that coiled oysters were found in muddy sediments and flat oysters in sandy sediments. The series was ecological, not evolutionary. Coiled oysters were better able to support themselves in mud, and the series of burial just depended on which life zone got buried first in an area

Internal mold of a clam

— muddy bottom or sandy bottom. The oysters lived in different places, not different times, and could be buried in either order. It was the environment that changed, not the oyster — just as Flood geologists would expect. Yet the flat-to-coiled oyster story was once considered one of the best "proofs" for evolution!

Clam

Perhaps the best mollusk evidence of creation and Flood geology are the shelled squids, like the nautilus. The modern pearly nautilus has a coiled shell with chambers. The squid-like animal lives in the last chamber; the other chambers regulate buoyancy so it can float at different depths without effort. Fossils with tapered, chambered shells are called nautiloids. Some are coiled like the modern nautilus, others are curved like bananas, and still others are straight, like ice cream cones.

Straight nautiloids enabled ICR geologist Dr. Steve Austin to document a catastrophic mass kill event preserved in a six-foot (2 m) layer near the base of the Grand Canyon's Redwall Limestone. Alignment of the shells enabled him to map the overwhelming current that killed and deposited about four billion nautiloids along a 150-mile (240 km) path from the east end of the Grand Canyon westward past Las Vegas, Nevada!

Nautiloid fossils are superb illustrations of the four Cs of biblical earth history. Nautiloids are among the most complex animals on earth, yet they are found at the bottom of the geologic column diagram in lowest Cambrian rock, evidence of complex beginnings — creation. Sadly, only the small pearly nautilus survives among a group which once included many large and varied forms — a record of death and decline in size and variety following the corruption of God's perfect world by man's sin. The burial of billions of nautiloids in a mass graveyard at the base of the Redwall Limestone in the Grand Canyon testifies to the catastrophe of Noah's flood. One or a few survivors of a once-great group, like the pearly nautilus, are called living fossils, and may remind us of the salvation we have in Christ, who came to save the faithful remnant of His people from worldwide judgment. So, nautiloids can be called missionary fossils, since you can share the whole gospel message just by telling people about the nautiloid fossils you find!

Evolutionists try to tell a story using nautiloids, too, a story based

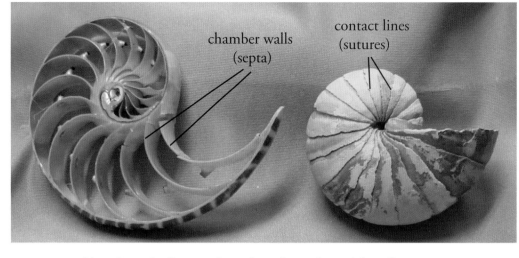

chamber walls (septa)

contact lines (sutures)

Nautilus shells, modern (sectioned) and fossil

on the contact lines (sutures) between the chamber walls (septa) and the shell. Although nautiloids have smooth sutures, those of cephalopods called ammonites are wiggly, as shown across the heading for chapter 4 on page 34. There is a stratigraphic series from smooth to slightly wiggly to more wiggly to very wiggly sutures, and this is often claimed to be the best fossil evidence for evolution.

Is the fossil sequence from smooth to very wiggly suture lines a good example of an evolutionary series? Absolutely not, for several reasons. First of all, the series starts with a very complex

Sea anemones (polyps)

animal at the bottom of the GCD, the opposite of the simple beginnings evolutionists had hoped to find. Second, the first-buried form is also the fittest, since it's the only survivor; the ammonites with the wiggly sutures all died out — the opposite of evolutionary progress! Third, the animal never evolved from anything or into anything; it started as a squid in a chambered shell and stayed a squid in a chambered shell. Fourth, there are few suggestions and no agreement on the survival value of having a wiggly suture (and those which had it died out). Fifth, there are reversals of the sequence evolutionists expected, forcing them to make up words like *pseudoammonite*. (*Pseudo* means "false," but it seems it's the evolutionary story, not the ammonite, that's false!)

It seems the four Cs of biblical earth history are the best guide to learning the truth about mollusk fossils, and mollusks are the second largest group of living things and the most abundant animal fossils of all!

Brain coral

Horn coral

Honeycomb coral

Varieties of coral

Staghorn coral

"Headless" Groups: Corals and Starfish

Water-filled animals that are each mostly a stomach and tentacles with stinging cells (nematocysts) belong to a group called either coelenterates or cnidarians. They come in two basic shapes — the umbrella shape called a jellyfish or medusa, or the can-with-fingers shape called a polyp. Soft-bodied forms are rare as fossils but include the impressions of jellyfish like those found in the Ediacara beds of South Australia (page 26, the ones evolutionists call the "oldest animal fossils in the world"). Soft polyps are often called sea anemones because they look like flowers and they come in a spectacular variety of colors and sizes.

Most polyps secrete a hard cup of calcium carbonate ($CaCO_3$) around their soft bodies. Polyps in hard cups are called corals. The cup of the horn coral looks like, as you might suspect, a cow or rhino horn. As the animal grew, the cup got wider, so horn corals probably looked like horns or ice cream cones with their points sticking down into the sea bottom. We can't be exactly sure, because horn corals seem to be extinct, which means no one has yet found any alive today.

Jellyfish (medusa)

Coral reef

Most corals still living today are colonial, which means they live cemented together in groups. The coral group may form a shape like a mound, a brain, a staghorn or elkhorn, or a huge reef. Along the shores of Lake Michigan near Petoskey, Michigan, cobble-sized fragments of fossil coral wash ashore in abundance, polished by wave action. In these Petoskey Stones or *Hexagonaria*, you can see the six-sided individual corals stuck together in a pattern like that of a honeycomb. Within each coral cup, walls (septa) extend from the outer edge toward the center in a pattern that makes the coral cup look like it has a hole in the center. These can be made into jewelry sold at rock shops, and antler-shaped staghorn and elkhorn corals are common in shell shops, too.

The biggest "apartment building" in the world is Australia's Great Barrier Reef, home to millions and millions of corals cemented together in ridges over 160 feet (50m) deep, stretching over 1,000 miles (1,600 km) along the Queensland coast. Another huge and beautiful chain of reefs, called the Florida Keys, stretches over 100 miles (160 km) from near Miami to Key West, Florida.

A cross (†) is often used to mark a grave in a cemetery, and paleontologists use a cross after the name of an organism or group to indicate that it's extinct, such as "horn corals (†)."

Extinction and decline in size and variety point back to the corruption of creation by man's sin and possibly to the tremendous environmental changes that followed the catastrophe of Noah's flood. Extinction is hard to prove, since we can't look everywhere at the same time! Fortunately, many animals once thought to be extinct have been found alive and well, usually in remote places. Maybe someday we'll find live horn corals. They were abundant in the pre-Flood world; some hillsides near Madison, Indiana, are so full of fossil horn corals that dozens can be picked up in just a few minutes!

Hexagonaria
(Petoskey stone)

What would have happened to reefs like these during Noah's flood? Sadly, they would have been broken up and destroyed. Fragments of huge reefs, including some big pieces over a mile (1.6 km) long have been found buried with other "seashells" in various systems of the geologic column — not growing in place, as evolutionists once believed, but catastrophically buried. Many deposits evolutionists once thought were reefs are actually shoals, huge amounts of shells all washed together and packed tightly, but not

Blastoids (sea buds)

columellas   stems

Crinoids (sea lilies)

cemented together like the organisms in a true reef. Buried reefs and shoals make good traps for oil, since there are lots of spaces between and within shells to hold oil, and the pores allow flow so the oil can be pumped out (after the initial pressure is released).

If pre-Flood reefs were destroyed and buried, is the 4,500–5,000 years since the Flood enough time to regrow the huge reefs like those of Australia and the Florida Keys? Yes! Australian scientists measuring modern reef growth at the slowest growing part of the Great Barrier Reef found rates of growth that would produce the entire 1,000 mile (1600 km) reef in only 3,700 years — at least 800 years to spare! It's been my pleasure to lead many student groups on scuba diving trips to the coral reefs off the Florida Keys. We have been able to see from year to year how fast corals grow back over damaged areas, or how fast they can cover a wreck. God told the people and animals getting off the ark to multiply and fill the earth, and apparently the corals obeyed God's command. God's purpose was to restore the earth, and corals quickly filled post-Flood environments suitable for them, which helped to make a home for many other creatures that are also part of the reef: various clams (including the giant *Tridacna*), stony sponges, algae, and members of the starfish (sea star) group.

Because they usually have bony plates and spines embedded in their skin, members of the starfish/sea star group are called echinoderms, meaning "spiny-skinned." Fossils of well-known, five-pointed sea stars are found, but other members of the group are far more commonly found.

It seems the pre-Flood world had areas with vast undersea gardens of upside-down starfish on stems called crinoids and blastoids (†). These animals are commonly called sea lilies and sea buds, because they had long, flexible "stems" supporting a star-patterned cup that looked like a flower or a bud, and "roots" that attached them to rocks or reefs — except that they could walk on their roots!

So many crinoid fossils are found in the Mississippian geologic system (GCD5) that evolutionists call it the Age of Crinoids.

Serpent stars

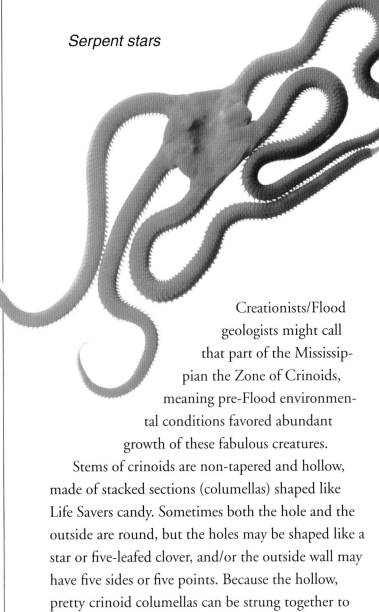

Creationists/Flood geologists might call that part of the Mississippian the Zone of Crinoids, meaning pre-Flood environmental conditions favored abundant growth of these fabulous creatures.

Stems of crinoids are non-tapered and hollow, made of stacked sections (columellas) shaped like Life Savers candy. Sometimes both the hole and the outside are round, but the holes may be shaped like a star or five-leafed clover, and/or the outside wall may have five sides or five points. Because the hollow, pretty crinoid columellas can be strung together to form necklaces, they are sometimes called Indian

beads. These fun-to-collect beads can be found in Indiana, Ohio, Iowa, Oklahoma, and other parts of central North America — far from the ocean today, but strong testimony that our continent was once under water!

Crinoid columellas are often found joined in short sections, and occasionally in long, twisted "ropes" like the spectacular crinoids from Le Grand, Iowa, displayed elegantly in the Natural History Museum in Des Moines. Cups of crinoids are harder to find than stems, but the cup of the sea bud (blastoid) is clear and dramatic. The five-pointed sea star pattern is exquisitely folded back on each bud (page 41). Crinoid cups may include branched arms, giving sea lilies another common name, feather stars.

Changes to the ocean environment after the Flood were apparently hard on crinoids and blastoids. Blastoids (†) are considered extinct, and the few survivors of the once-great crinoid group are living fossils — a testimony to corruption and decline, not evolution. Surviving crinoids, like those I've seen while scuba diving Australia's Great Barrier Reef, still show eye-popping colors and a beauty of form that reminds us both of God's wondrous creation and Christ's preservation of a remnant (page 77). In other words, crinoids make great missionary fossils, just as nautiloids and clams do.

Sand dollars and sea urchins are other members of the starfish group (echinoderms) commonly found as fossils. Mary found sea urchin spines in a Florida fossil site famous for its forest and grassland animals, perhaps suggesting the sea covered even these environments.

Serpent stars and sea cucumbers are different from most other echinoderms. Most echinoderms use suction cups on a stalk (tube feet) for walking.

Fossil of crinoid cup and tentacles

The serpent star thrashes its arms so they look like snakes or worms, and they can shed them, like a lizard sheds its tail, to distract predators. The sea cucumber does something even more astonishing to distract predators; it empties out all its internal organs into a tasty, colorful pile! Then the hollow body crawls away to grow back all its internal organs — including a respiratory tree that allows it to breathe through its rear digestive opening (its anus, instead of its mouth)!

Sand dollars, sea urchins, and urchin spines

Arthropods

Arthropod means "jointed (*arthro-*) leg (-*pod*)." Arthropoda is the largest phylum (animal group) by far. It includes all creatures with jointed legs and a tough outside skeleton (exoskeleton) made of chitin: insects, crabs and shrimp, spiders, centipedes, and millipedes.

Live insects are all too common, but fossil insects are rare, largely because their armor of chitin breaks up and decomposes easily at death. Insects can be preserved in delicate detail in hardened pine sap (amber, see page 12), and in certain fine-grained siltstones and claystones (shales), such as parts of the Green River Shale in Wyoming, the Florissant Fossil Beds in Colorado, and the Burgess Shale in the Canadian Rockies.

The Florissant Beds high in the Colorado Rockies contain fossilized flies and mosquitoes.

When these fossils are viewed under a microscope, the veins in the flies' wings, the tiny balancing organs (halteres) behind the wings, facets in the compound eyes, and even bristles on the feet can be seen! It's possible that poisons released into the water from volcanic action prevented breakdown by bacteria and scavengers, and a chemical (a flocculent) caused the silt and clay to settle quickly in briefly quiet water, solidifying fast enough to prevent later currents from tearing apart the fragile specimens. Since water itself decomposes the arthropod body, it would be impossible for such creatures to be preserved slowly and gradually over millions of years!

Like fossils in amber, the arthropod fossils in shale contradict evolution and provide powerful support for creation. The creatures preserved are almost identical to those still living (although some, like a dragonfly with a 27-inch [68 cm] wing spread, were much bigger). Roaches are roaches; ants are ants; ticks are ticks; spiders are spiders; and so forth — each well designed to multiply after its kind (creation) right from the moment of its first burial or lowest preservation in the fossil sequence. There are not even any popular evolutionary stories about how the wings, eyes, and other special features of the arthropod groups evolved — and no evidence that they evolved at all!

The most famous of all arthropod fossils are the terrific trilobites. Stratigraphically, they are the first creatures to be found in abundance as fossils. They were found in sea-bottom environments all around the pre-Flood world, yet they seem to be mysteriously extinct today for reasons that puzzle paleontologists as much as the extinction of dinosaurs.

Trilobites make good fossils partly because they

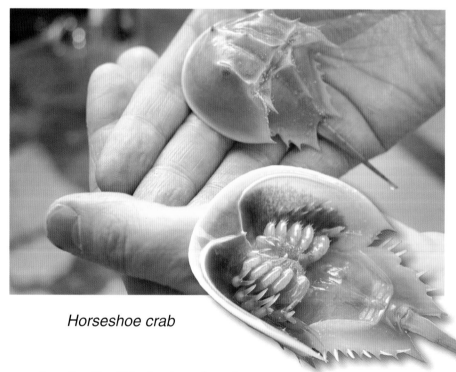

Horseshoe crab

were "pre-fossilized" by having a lot of CaCO$_3$ (lime) hardening their chitin armor. It seems they shoveled through sand and mud on the sea bottom, like horseshoe crabs do today, so they were already partly buried as well as pre-fossilized

when the Flood sediments began to pile up on top of them and the horseshoe crabs.

Horseshoe crabs survive, unchanged (unevolved) since their first appearance in the GCD and are among the living fossils. The larval (immature) stage of the horseshoe crab is called a trilobite larva, and probably gives us a clue as to what live trilobites were like. Evolutionists think trilobites have been extinct for 200 million years or so, but they thought some animals called graptolites living in chitin cups had been extinct for 500 million years — until some were found alive and well in the Indian Ocean west of Australia! So, I still hold out hope some trilobites may yet be found alive. Tracks similar to fossilized trilobite tracks have been reported in deep-ocean sediment.

Trilobites are the first animals fossilized in abundance and mark lowest Cambrian at the bottom of the GCD, but my paleontology teacher, an evolutionist, said, "Never let anyone say a trilobite is a simple animal." Arthropods are tied with squids as the most complex of all animals without backbones (invertebrates), and trilobites are complex arthropods! A trilobite's body is divided into three sections: a head (cephalon), usually with antennae (feelers) and awesome eyes; a many-legged thorax (body) whose sections are each divided into three lobes ("tri-lobed"); and a tail (pygidium).

The trilobite's compound eye is a scientific marvel. Each section (facet) has a double lens system for precise underwater vision. Scuba divers and snorkelers have to be reminded that to a diver with a face mask, things underwater look bigger and closer than they really are. The trilobite did not have that vision problem; it saw things as they really were. Scientists couldn't make a lens like that until recent times, yet God gave this fantastic lens to the humble (but not simple) trilobite. Once again, the lesson is complex beginnings — creation not evolution. The decline and death of such fabulous creatures remind us also of corruption and catastrophe.

Trilobites come in a fascinating variety of sizes and shapes, including at least one (*Flexicalymene*) that can roll up in a ball (like a roly-poly or pill bug). Trilobites are fun to collect and interesting to show to people. They can be collected from sites such as the hillsides of Indiana, Ohio, and Kentucky; the plains of Kansas and Nebraska; the mountains of California; the Australian island state of Tasmania; and quarries in Sweden and England.

It's great to find a whole trilobite, of course, but finding parts is also fun, and lets you know you're in an area where you might find whole ones. Typical parts include: heads and partial heads without "cheeks," thorax sections, tails, tri-lobed thorax cross-sections, and a "mouth plate" (hypostome) from under the head.

The Utica Shale in New York is a special trilobite deposit that includes mostly legs and antennae. This indicates the action of flowing water sorting things out into layers by shape and density. Obviously, trilobite legs and antennas did not evolve in a time zone different from the rest of the trilobite!

Superb preservation of intricate detail is found among trilobites preserved in the famous mid-Cambrian Burgess Shale in the Canadian Rockies.

Several creatures looking strange to us are preserved with the trilobites, including a form (*Asheiya*) that looks a lot like the Australian rain forest creature called *Peripatus*.

Peripatus, the "railroad worm," has features usually seen separately in the insect group (arthropods) and the earthworm group (annelids).

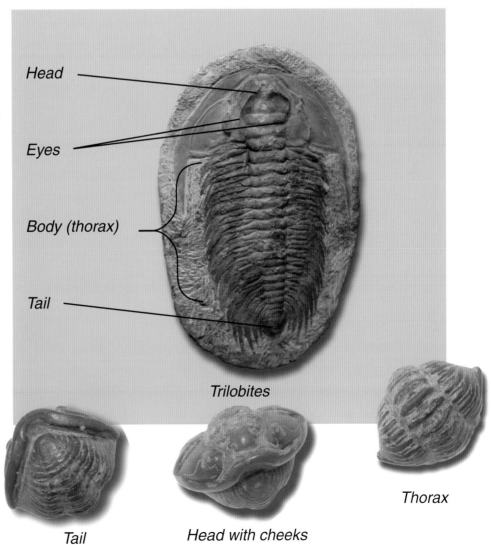

Head

Eyes

Body (thorax)

Tail

Trilobites

Tail

Head with cheeks

Thorax

Peripatus

It has a complex system of air tubes (tracheae) with multiple openings and a circulatory system without capillaries, two traits it shares with insects. It has a worm-like body and non-jointed fleshy appendages like some members of the earthworm group. Could it be a missing link between arthropods and annelids? No.

Peripatus cannot be considered the ancestor of either annelids (earthworm group) or arthropods, since both these groups had varied and complex members living and dying before even the mid-Cambrian *Peripatus*-like form was buried. Furthermore, the separate traits are complete and complex, neither simple traits nor halfway traits like a missing link should have. A unique combination of non-unique traits seems to qualify *Peripatus* as a distinct created kind. It has a special glue-spitting gland that sets it apart, too. Any difficulties in classifying it result from problems with man's grouping, not God's design.

The first land animals found as fossils as we go up the GCD are arthropods. They are not simple animals that are just barely arthropods. Instead, they belong to complex specialized arthropod groups, including centipedes, insects called silverfish, and mites. There is no evidence they evolved from simpler animals lower in the column. They are simply the first land animals trapped as the rising waters of Noah's flood began to bury animals above the pre-Flood shoreline.

Lampshells and Moss Animals

Two groups of seashells are so common as fossils that they are called fossil weeds. The first group, lampshells or brachiopods, are bivalves like clams, but the animal inside is quite different. The two shells of brachs are usually unequal and top and bottom, not equal and right and left as they are in clams.

Brachiopods use muscles and a pulley system to open their shells, so fossil brachs are usually found with their two shells closed together, unlike clams.

The brach shell is harder than the clamshell (calcite vs. aragonite), so the brach is usually preserved with much more detail than the mold of a clamshell.

Brachs come in a variety of sizes and shapes, usually well preserved, so they are fun to collect and easy to identify from picture keys. One type of brach looks like an Aladdin's lamp, giving the group the common name lampshells. The hole that looks like the lamp's opening

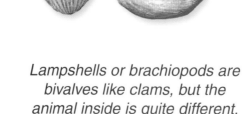

Lampshells or brachiopods are bivalves like clams, but the animal inside is quite different.

is found in the bottom shell of all brachs, and a fleshy stalk extends through it in live animals.

Brachs are very common in Paleozoic (early-Flood) rock, less common in Mesozoic (mid-Flood) rock, and scarce in Cenozoic (late-Flood and post-Flood) deposits and in oceans today. Clams, the other bivalve filter feeders, show the opposite trend. They are less common at the bottom of the GCD and more common at the top and in modern waters. It seems like environmental conditions favored brachs in the pre-Flood world and clams in the post-Flood.

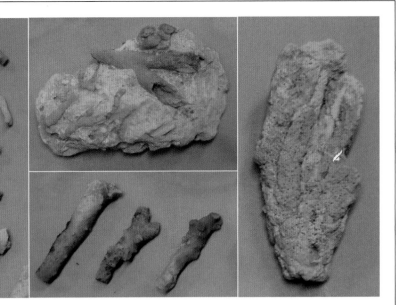

Bryozoans

Archimedes, *the corkscrew bryozoan*

Brachs are sometimes included with living fossils because there were so many varieties in the past and so few survive today. However, the "champion animal" is a brach, the spatula-shaped *Lingula. Lingula* has remained so unchanged ("un-evolved") that it's given the same name from Cambrian to recent, the longest stratigraphic range for any scientific name. The secret of *Lingula's* success? Stick in the mud, open your mouth (shells) slightly to eat, and mind your own business! By evolutionary standards, *Lingula* is the fittest of all animals, the longest survivor. Creationists point out *Lingula* just followed God's command to multiply after kind!

The other group called fossil weeds are the moss animals or bryozoans. Bryozoans are animals with tentacles that live in limestone cups like corals do. Though much smaller than the coral animal, the bryozoan animal is much more complex. It has a brain and nerves, heart and blood vessels, muscles,

and a complete digestive system — mouth, esophagus, stomach, intestines, and anus. (In some bryozoans known as ectoprocts, the anus opens outside the arm of tentacles [*ecto* means "out"]; in the entoprocts, it opens inside [*ento* means "in"].)

One bryozoan, *Bugula*, does something totally astonishing. First, it looks like it's dying. It shrivels up into a little "brown body" of goo in the bottom of its cup. However, it leaves behind a few living cells that begin to grow up and around the brown body, building a new animal with new brain, heart, muscles, stomach, and every other necessary feature. The brown-body goo of the first animal winds up in the stomach of the new animal and gets spit out! Did you ever feel like you would like to wad yourself up, spit yourself out, and start all over again?

Limestone cups cemented into moss animal colonies make good fossils in a variety of shapes. Some form flat, lacy, checkerboard patterns, like bryozoan colonies living on kelp "leaves" (blades) along the coast of California. Others form mounds, or mounds with stalks like mushrooms. Many form staghorn shapes. Bryozoan mounds and staghorn colonies have tiny holes widely spaced, while coral mounds and staghorns have bigger holes more closely spaced, and the coral holes have septa (partitions). The stalk of one bryozoan, called *Archimedes*, is shaped like a corkscrew, and it's an index to Mississippian rock (GCD5).

Bryozoans are found throughout the geologic column and are still living today. No evolution here!

Sponges and Microfossils

Not all sponges are soft and squishy — the kinds that are harvested as bath sponges are, but there are many species that have hard skeletal structures of crystal-like spines called spicules. When the sponge body rots or dissolves, the spicules are left behind. Their spectacular beauty can be seen under the microscope, but the beauty can be deceiving; they

Sponge spicules

are sometimes as sharp as slivers of glass.

In the southwest corner of Australia, we hunted fossils in a hill made mostly of sponge spicules compressed to form "spongillite" rock. The spongillite hill showed how powerful currents in Noah's flood could sort out structures and bury them in huge piles!

Sponge spicules are made by incredible living cells called amebocytes. The spicule starts off inside the amebocyte cell. As it gets too big for one cell, the amebocyte divides — clones itself — to make helpers. The helpers work from the tips of the spicule arms, keeping just the right distances and angles from each other, decorating the end of each spine. In addition, amebocytes can change themselves into egg and sperm cells for sexual reproduction; they can build and decorate special structures called gemmules to carry the sponge over harsh conditions and/or to reproduce the sponge asexually; they capture food from the inside of the sponge and use it to feed cells on the outside; and if a sponge gets squashed, they can put it back together again. Never let anyone tell you a sponge is a simple animal that just evolved by chance!

The microscope or magnifying glass reveals many tiny fossils called microfossils. The microscopic spores and pollen of plants are studied in a branch of paleontology called palynology. Some one-celled animals, called protozoans, have shells. Limestone deposits called chalk are made

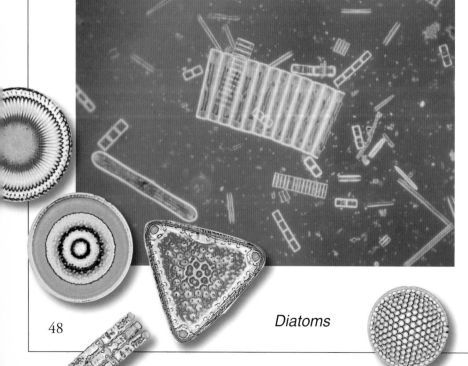

Diatoms

48

of the carbonate ($CaCO_3$) shells of countless numbers of foram protozoans. Some protozoans, called radiolarians, have shells made of glass (SiO_2). The chalk used to write on blackboards is made of foram shells; the annoying screeching sound is made by glassy radiolarians.

Many paleontologists work for oil companies. They study forams (shelled amoebas) in rock cuttings and in cylinders of rock brought up by drilling (well cores) and use the information to map underground layers of rock. Ostracodes, called fossil jellybeans, are tiny bivalve arthropods also used in underground mapping. Tiny, young stages of clams and snails also help, as do fragments of other seashells and sponge spicules.

Diatoms are microscopic, one-celled plants whose walls are decorated with glass (SiO_2) in exquisite patterns (page 48). The Flood sometimes washed huge piles of diatoms together in a common graveyard. The glassy fragments are mined and sold as diatomaceous earth, which is used in filtering and abrasion. Near Lompoc, California, microfossils were dumped so rapidly and in such a great quantity that they trapped and preserved the bones of a huge whale. The whale could not have been trapped, of course, if the diatoms accumulated only a little bit at a time over millions of years.

Some diatoms in thick deposits may have been alive during Noah's flood. Others may have died

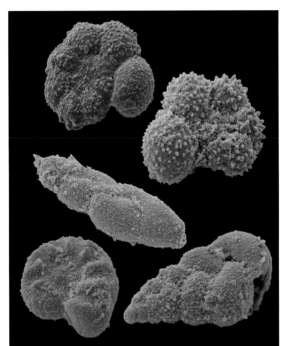

Fossilized foraminiferans ("forams") as seen with the scanning electron microscope (SEM).

before the Flood and been lying in the sea bottom, along with forams, radiolarians, and other microfossils, forming oozes. Oozes, or squishy layers of tiny shells and fragments, form on the sea bottom today.

Seashell fossils cover the earth, up to the tops of the highest mountains — evidence that points back clearly to the worldwide flood at Noah's time. After 150 days (5 months), the Bible tells us, "all the high hills under the whole heavens" were covered with water (Gen. 7:19). Then, as Psalm 104:8 tells us, "The mountains rose, and the valleys sank down." At the end of the Flood, God raised up the layers that were below the sea, lifting sea-creature fossils even to the tops of earth's highest mountains, the Himalayas. The waters ran off the land for another 150 days (5 months), eroding some of the layers and leaving a few bare patches of granite on the continents.

Truly, Noah's flood was an awesome judgment for man's sin, but God provided a way of escape, the ark, for all who would repent and turn to Him. The Bible tells us man's sin now will bring a final judgment by fire. Once again, God provides a way of escape for those who ask forgiveness and accept salvation through His Son, Jesus Christ. Jesus said that at His final coming, the earth would be "as it was in the days of Noah" (Matt. 24:37–39). Be sure you're safely in the arms of Jesus!

CHAPTER FIVE
KINDS OF FOSSILS II: VERTEBRATES

Animals with backbones are called vertebrates. They include fish, amphibians (frogs and salamanders), reptiles (snakes, turtles, lizards, and dinosaurs), birds, and mammals (cats, dogs, rabbits, bears). Probably because people have many features in common with vertebrates, most museums display lots of vertebrate fossils, even though the vast majority of fossils are invertebrates, especially seashells.

Invertebrate fossils are found almost everywhere; vertebrate fossils are found in abundance only in special locations. Seashell fossils are often found complete, well preserved, and easy to identify; vertebrate fossils are often just fragments of bones and teeth, incomplete, often poorly preserved, and hard to identify, but when you find a good bone or tooth, it's great!

Fish

Parts of fish found as fossils include scales, spines, backbones (vertebrae), and mouth parts. Whole fish fossils are often flattened carbon films (above). In many areas, such as Fossil Butte National Monument in Wyoming, huge numbers of fossil fish are found buried together, all pointing in roughly the same direction. That shows the fish were all washed in at the same time by one gigantic current, not buried slowly at random over millions of years. In a few cases, a big fish is fossilized with the little fish it was eating still caught in its mouth! It certainly didn't take millions of years to form those fossils!

Evolutionists have never been able to agree on any theory about how fish evolved or from what invertebrate group. The fossil evidence shows that fish have always been fish, from the few Cambrian fish found up to those living today. Fish with skeletons of cartilage, like sharks, are found higher in the stratigraphic sequence than fish with bony skeletons. That's another puzzle for evolutionists, since bone

develops from cartilage, they had hoped to find cartilage fish buried before, not after, bony fish.

Fossil shark teeth are highly prized in the area where we live (southwest Florida). A student of mine found one five inches (nearly 13 cm) along its edge. It was a "meg," an extinct shark, *Carcharodon megalodon*. The Carolinas are also known for huge shark teeth. Some reach nearly eight inches (20 cm), suggesting a shark over 80 feet (over 25 m) long — twice the largest known today!

Carcharodon megalodon teeth

Amphibians

Amphibian means "double life." Amphibians, like frogs and salamanders, lead two lives: the first as a tadpole with gills that eats plants, the second as an adult with lungs that usually eats insects.

Amphibians have the most DNA per cell of any animal, and even more than human beings. They have all the instructions for living in water and eating plants and all those for living on land and eating insects — plus all the instructions for making the spectacular change (called metamorphosis) from tadpole into adult. Sadly, in our fallen world, even with all the right genes spelling out the plan ahead of time, many tadpoles die in trying to make the change from water to land. Yet unbelievably, evolutionists claim at least one fish made the change from water to land just by chance, without the right genes! (Better make that two fish, male and female, each having "miracle mutations" in the same place at the same time!)

To support their claim that fish evolved into amphibians by time, chance, struggle, and death — all

without God's design — evolutionists once offered the coelacanth. Fossils showed the creature had bones in its front fins, vaguely like the bones in the arm of a frog or human being. Artistic drawings even showed the fin bent with an elbow and hands. It was claimed the fins changing to legs enabled the creature to win the struggle for survival by crawling from ponds that dried up to ponds with water.

Then the coelacanth (next page), thought to be extinct for millions of years, was found alive and well! Fishermen in the Comores Islands in the Indian Ocean had been catching them and eating them for years! Another group has recently been found in ocean waters near Indonesia. The living coelacanth completely contradicted the evolutionists' story. There were no elbow or wrist

Parker grandchildren in megalodon *jaw*

joints; the stiff fin was used for steering and swimming, not walking. This fish did not live in ponds; it lived in the deep ocean. Their organs worked more like those in a shark, not those in a frog.

Frustrated evolutionists now try to use living fish to support their view, but science won't help them. The mudskipper can "walk" on land (and even climb twigs in search of insects), but it has no lungs and no bones in its fins. Florida's walking catfish wriggles across land using its spines, not its fins. So-called lungfish have swim bladders they can use to absorb oxygen from air, but they have tiny fins that can't help them crawl anywhere. When their pond dries up, they burrow into the mud and secrete a waterproof cocoon that dissolves when the pond fills again. All these are examples of amazing designs that help God's creatures live in special environments, but none of them support evolution. The animals are designed for transitional (in-between) water/land environments, but it's the environments, not the animals, that are transitional.

Amphibian leg vs. coelacanth fin

Coelacanth

The "first" amphibian fossils found in the GCD also embarrased evolutionists. They are not simple creatures, half-fish, half-frog. Instead, they are much bigger than modern amphibians (imagine a 4 foot or 1.2 m frog!) with very complex skull bones and a complete set of four legs that look nothing like fins! This is not a record of evolution, but a record of design, followed by decline in size and variety.

Reptiles

Snakes, turtles, lizards, alligators, and dinosaurs are all examples of reptiles. Calling an animal a reptile is a shorthand way of saying it has a skin covered with scales and reproduces its kind by laying shelled eggs.

The eggs of reptiles and birds are incredible things. The little baby grows from a single cell inside a protective, water-filled sac called the amnion (so the egg is called amniote). Its food for energy and body building is supplied by fats in the yolk (the yellow) and proteins in the albumen (the white). Waste products are stored in the allantois.

All these parts are wrapped up in an awesome shell, either hard or leathery, that has a membrane and pores just perfect for letting oxygen in, keeping germs out, keeping water (H_2O) in, while at the same time letting carbon dioxide (CO_2) out.

The next time you eat an egg, take time to think about how marvelously God designed it, not just about how good it tastes.

Eggs can be found as fossils. In the past few years, many dinosaur eggs have been found in China and Argentina. Some have the bones of little baby dinosaurs inside! The biggest dinosaurs known to science hatched from eggs smaller than footballs, and most hatched from much smaller eggs! That means that when a giant long-necked dinosaur, like *Apatosaurus* or *Brachiosaurus* or the biblical behemoth (Job 40:15–24) hatched out of its egg, it was small enough that someone could hold it, pet it, even put a string around its neck and take it for a walk! A baby *T. rex* could have perched on someone's shoulder like a parrot!

Yikes, you might be thinking, even a baby *T. rex* would have teeth sharp enough and big enough to bite my ear off — or worse! However, many animals with sharp, pointed teeth today are just vegetarians. Over 80 percent of the diet of grizzly bears is plant material; polar bears in the San Diego Zoo love carrots and lettuce; and pandas, with teeth like the other bears, only eat bamboo. Remember, God created all animals and people in the beginning to eat only plants. It was only after man's sin corrupted God's perfect creation that some animals began to eat other animals, and it was only after the Flood that God gave mankind permission to eat meat.

Baby dinosaurs were big enough to hold in your hand, as seen in this photo of a fossilized dinosaur egg.

Teeth tend to make superb fossils because they have a very hard coating (enamel) that doesn't break down easily. They also come in a wide variety of shapes and sizes and often have intricate swirls, bumps (cusps), and other design patterns that provide paleontologists with lots of detail. Finding a tooth with a special pattern often serves, like a fingerprint, to identify the whole animal (see page 76). Sometimes scientists get over-excited (like other human beings) and try to make up a whole new creature from a single tooth. An overzealous evolutionist, for example, once built a picture of Nebraska Man, *"Hesperopithecus,"* his wife, family, and society from a single tooth — a tooth later discovered to belong to a fossil pig!

Remember, too, that sharp, pointed teeth, even ones with saw-like edges (serrations), do not necessarily mean a meat-eating (carnivorous) diet. Serrated knives are used to cut bread and tomatoes as well as meat. The serrated edges of many shark teeth, coupled with the shark's side-to-side head motions, can certainly tear up a seal, but the same teeth and behavior would be great for grazing on the ocean's forests of nutritious kelp.

Claws, horns, and scales are made or covered with keratin, the protein that also makes up our hair and fingernails. Keratin rots more easily than bone, so claws, horns, and scales are somewhat rare as fossils. Scales may also be preserved as impressions in rock, and scaly skin impressions of dinosaurs have

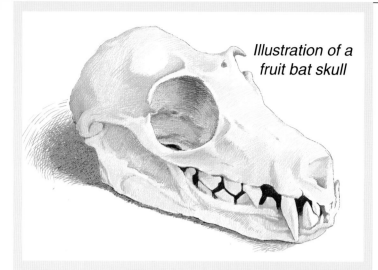

*Illustration of a
fruit bat skull*

*Sharp teeth and claws can be used
(as God originally designed them)
just to eat plants. The fruit bat's teeth
(above) rip and slash into mangoes
and papayas. The claws of the giant
ground sloth (below) act as a leaf
rake. Like hawks, parrots have strong
hooked bills and sharp talons, but they
only eat seeds.*

Claw core from a giant ground sloth

been found. Like teeth, claws are not indications of diet. Huge, powerful claws may belong to a meat eater (e.g., crocodile), to an animal that eats fruits and vegetables (e.g., iguana), or to one that eats roots and/or digs burrows (e.g., some turtles). Some claws, horns, and scales have a bony core that preserves better than keratin, and pieces (scutes) of alligator armor and turtle shell are common as fossils in certain places.

Fossil claws and teeth can't tell you what an animal ate, but coprolites can. You may remember (pages 13–14) that coprolites are fossil feces (animal droppings). Slicing, polishing, and examining a coprolite will reveal bits of twigs and leaves for a plant eater, or pieces of broken bone for a carnivore.

Fossil reptiles seem to offer strong support to 4C creationists, not to evolutionists. Lizards, snakes, turtles, and crocodiles found as fossils look like lizards, snakes, turtles, and crocodiles today — except there was a greater variety of kinds and larger sizes among reptiles in the past than the present. The reptiles were obviously well designed to multiply after their kinds (creation), followed by a decline in size and variety (corruption and catastrophe), with a remnant of the past preserved (Christ) as living fossils, such as the Komodo dragon and the tuatara.

Even dinosaurs make great missionary fossils! Land dinosaurs would have been created on day 6 and walked the pre-Flood earth with mankind. That may sound scary, but think about this: the average dinosaur was only the size of a big dog or small pony; many were only the size of chickens. Only a few got to be really huge, but the very largest would take up only half the space (volume) of a great blue whale. Even the huge ones hatched out of eggs you could hold in one hand! Besides, many dinosaurs, even after man's sin ruined God's world, were vegetarian. People in India live with elephants that are larger than most dinosaurs, but they live in harmony and keep elephants to help around the farm! So, living with dinosaurs is not as frightening as *Jurassic Park* would make you think.

So, what happened to the dinosaurs? Many dinosaurs, like other animals, were buried in Noah's flood, often in huge fossil graveyards, and their bones turned to fossil stone. The presence of protein, DNA, and even blood cells in some of these bones tells us that dinosaur fossils are only thousands of years old at most, not millions.

If dinosaurs were around to get fossilized in Noah's flood 4,500–5,000 years ago, weren't two of every kind of land dinosaur on the ark? Wouldn't the ark just sink if an *Ultrasaurus* stepped on board? Not at all, for two reasons: (1) the ark was a whole lot bigger than we often think — about 450 feet long, 75 feet wide, and 45 feet high (in meters, a little less than 150 x 25 x 15), according to the Bible, and (2) dinosaurs are much smaller than we usually imagine. Noah could have taken dinosaur eggs, but that would be cheating. God wanted dinosaurs to multiply and fill the earth again, so he probably brought to Noah young adults ready for reproduction. A 100-foot (30 m) brachiosaur that hatched from its egg at one foot (30 cm) in length was likely a reproductively mature adult at 15–20 feet (6 m). The figure in the bottom right corner shows a full-grown man with a young adult dinosaur of the largest kind. There was plenty of room on the ark, not for just two dinosaurs, but for two of each of the created dinosaur kinds!

If dinosaurs got on the ark, they got off the ark. Probably two things happened then. First, as we'll discuss later, climate and soil conditions changed dramatically after the Flood, and these changes in plants and environments seemed to make survival harder for all

amphibians and reptiles, but especially dinosaurs. Second, many scientists, including some evolutionists, tell us that over-hunting by people brought animals bigger than most dinosaurs to extinction in just the last 4,000 years, and it's likely many dinosaurs met the same fate.

Five Christian adventurers brought back 200 pounds (90 kg) of fresh, unfossilized dinosaur bones from the North Slope of Alaska. These dinosaurs had certainly not been dead for 65 million years, or the fresh bones would have rotted away. Rock paintings, carvings, and stories from many cultures record encounters with animals whose descriptions match those of known kinds of dinosaurs. Crocodiles appear in the rock record before dinosaurs and include specimens that weighed more than *T. rex*; they persist today despite dramatic climate change and over-hunting, and perhaps even a remnant of the dinosaur group will yet be found.

Birds

Prized for their beauty, grace, and feats of flight, birds are defined as creatures possessing one of God's most familiar yet awesome designs, the feather.

DINOSAURS: MISSIONARY FOSSILS

Creation

Like snakes, turtles, and alligators, dinosaurs first appear in the geologic column complete and complex as separate and distinct kinds, well designed to multiply after their kinds.

Corruption

Dinosaurs illustrate death and decline in size and variety in a sin-ruined world, the opposite of evolution.

Catastrophe

Graveyards of dinosaur fossils show they were buried fast and deep in huge Flood deposits, and perhaps also in post-Flood sediments.

Christ

Fresh dinosaur bones and historical records show God preserved dinosaurs on the ark so that they began to multiply over the earth after the Flood. Even some evolutionists believe dinosaurs may survive as living fossils in remote parts of the world today.

A flight feather consists of a shaft that develops from a bump of blood-rich tissue at the base of a pit, the follicle, sunk deep in the skin. The shaft produces pairs of branches in a plane, the barbs. The barbs are joined front-to-back by hook-and-eyelet connectors called the barbules. Birds run their bills up and down their feathers, unzippering and rezippering the barbules, cleaning, oiling, and realigning their barbs as they preen.

Feathers are often highly colored. Pigments are "painted" on barbs in different places to create beautiful patterns, some even looking three-dimensional. Patterns vary from one part of the bird to another, and from one created kind to another. Some colors are caused not by paint (pigments) but by diffraction and by the prism effect (the way light is bent or refracted as it passes through sections of clear keratin protein with special shapes). Colors are even produced by the same effect (interference) that produces the shimmering rainbow of colors in a film of oil. God is indeed the Master Artist as well as the Master Designer!

Evolutionists teach that feathers evolved from scales, but nothing could be further from the scientific truth. Like our hair and fingernails, scales and feathers are made of keratin protein, but that's where the resemblance ends. Scales of fish, reptiles, and birds are sheets of keratin produced in the upper layer of skin by growth in expanding rings — not at all like the feather's shaft with branches (barbs) joined by hooks-and-eyelets (barbules) that develop from pits (follicles) deep within the skin. Paleontologists have found fossils of scales and fossils of feathers, but no one has ever found a fossil "sceather," something in-between a scale and a feather. If evolution were true, there would once have been millions of animals with billions of "sceathers" and some should have been found by now.

In fact, eager desire to find a missing link between reptiles and birds produced two of evolution's more famous mistakes, *Archaeopteryx* and National Geographic's "dino-bird." *Archaeopteryx* has probably been used more than any other fossil to fool people into believing evolution. (I used it on my students

Beauty in feathers: God's artistry

claws on its wings; the penguin has a bony tail and unfused backbones; several fossil birds had teeth. Besides that, there were no in-between (transitional) traits. The feathers were feathers, not "sceathers" between scales and feathers. The wings were wings, not half-leg/half-wing. In fact, the wings and feathers were like those of a strong flyer, and *Archaeopteryx* also had a strong wishbone (furcula) like strong flyers have. Science has forced paleontologists to conclude *Archaeopteryx* was a strong flying bird, not at all a missing link.

In fact, the *Archaeopteryx* specimens we have could not be the ancestors of birds simply because regular (more familiar) birds are found lower in the geologic column than *Archae-opteryx* (Triassic vs. Jurassic, GCD8 vs. GCD9). An evolutionist might argue that someday *Archaeopteryx* fossils will be found lower in the column, and that's okay — so long as the evolutionist admits that belief is based on blind faith and not scientific discovery!

when I believed in evolution!) It was reported from a German limestone quarry in 1861, just two years after Darwin's book on survival of the fittest admitted that "intermediate links" were "perhaps the most obvious and serious objection to the theory" of evolution. The specimen, about crow size, had a long, bony tail; backbones not fused together; claws on its wings; and teeth in its bill — all features most people associate with reptiles and not birds. The specimen also had detailed impressions of feathers on its wings and tail. "Eureka!" exclaimed the evolutionist. "We have a perfect example of a link between reptiles and birds!"

Then science disproved evolution's overzealous claim. The features thought to make *Archaeopteryx* reptilian are found in other birds: the ostrich has

Archaeopteryx

Wings are fantastic structures, of course, with bones named like those in front legs, but arranged in strikingly different patterns. If legs evolved into wings, paleontologists should have found all the in-between stages by now. Fossils have been found of only wings or legs with nothing in-between — and that's true not only for birds but for the other three great groups of flyers as well: flying mammals (bats), flying reptiles (pterodactyls), and flying insects (flies, dragonflies, butterflies). It looks like wings were designed as wings, complete and complex, right from their creation!

You may have seen or heard about the *National Geographic* article (Nov. 1999), "Feathers for *T. rex*?" With the beautiful pictures for which it's known, *Geographic* described a fossil "dinosaur-bird" from China, complete with astonishing details of its feathers. In an open letter to the public, bird expert Storrs Olson of the famous Smithsonian Institute called *Geographic*'s "dino-bird" claim "sensationalistic, unsubstantiated tabloid journalism" (in the same category as humans giving birth to aliens). He was right. Three months later — after over 100,000 students had gone through National Geographic's exhibit — paleontologists had proven the fossil was a fake put together by a Chinese local from pieces of fossil birds and fossil reptiles.

When you see *National Geographic* making some other claim for evolution in the future (and I am fairly sure you will!), just remember to wait until the scientific evidence is in before making up your mind! So far, the fossil evidence is telling us that birds have always been birds, just as the Bible says. Evolution stories come and go, but evidence continues to build up supporting the biblical record of history — "His story"!

If you ever find a fossil bird bone, treasure it. Many bird bones are smoothly hollow, designed to contain a lung sac for the bird's unique and amazing high-powered "flow-through" breathing system. This hollow-yet-strong and lightweight construction is also superbly designed for flight — but not for preservation as a fossil, so bird bones are somewhat rare.

Mammals

Animals with hair or fur that nourish their young on milk are called mammals. Mammals include many familiar pet, farm, zoo, and wild animals — dogs, cats, horses, cattle, giraffes, elephants, bears, and deer. Included also are aquatic (or marine) mammals (like whales, dolphins, and manatees), pouched mammals (marsupials, like kangaroos and koalas), and a few egg-laying mammals (monotremes, like the platypus). Famous fossil mammals include the woolly mammoths (hairy elephants) preserved in Arctic ice and in cave paintings; the saber-toothed cat *(Smilodon)* found in California's La Brea Tar Pits along with remains of people; and the giant ground sloth that was bigger than *T. rex*.

Most areas rich in dinosaur fossils are off limits to amateur collectors, but there are many places to hunt awesome mammal remains. One of the best is the Peace River which flows

Saber-toothed cat skull

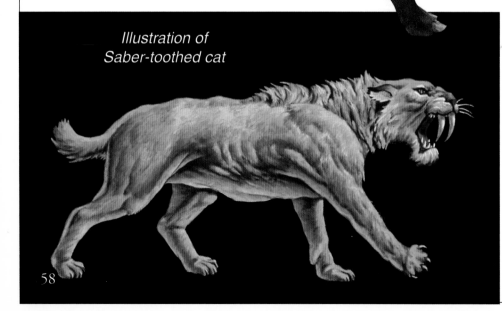

Illustration of Saber-toothed cat

Alligator scutes

Horse teeth

Turtle scutes

Sea cow ribs

Camel leg bone

right past the Creation Adventures Museum in Arcadia, Florida, where we live and work. Mary helped to plaster jacket what turned out to be the largest femur (upper rear leg bone) of a Columbian mammoth ever found. We also take students and families on fossil hunting canoe trips along the Peace River. Big fossils (below) must be properly excavated, but some fossils (left) can be screened from sand in the river. Similar fossils can also be found in shell pits, quarries with billions of beautiful fossil shells mined for road bases in Florida.

Look again at the pictures of fossils from Florida rivers and shell pits. In the same rock, same layer of shells, or same bank of sand, you can find fossils of large land animals (mammoths, giant

Mammoth femur

Mammoth jaw and teeth

ground sloths, giant armadillos, camels, llamas, saber-toothed cats) buried with large sea creatures (whales, walruses, manatees, great white, and many other huge sharks). Paleontologists often call Florida's sedimentary deposits "fossil hash." What produced Florida's fossil hash, with big land and sea creatures from different environments all mixed together? The answer may be a catastrophe of ice and super-storms that probably followed Noah's flood.

Scientists recognize evidence that shows the earth once had a warm climate from pole to pole, with fossils of alligators and palm trees and/or subtropical vegetation found near both North and South Poles. Most scientists think the earth once had much more carbon dioxide (CO_2) than its present 0.03 percent. H_2O and CO_2 act like the glass in a greenhouse to "bottle up" heat from the sun. During the Flood, the $CaCO_3$ in fossil bones, shells, and limestone would be kept from releasing its CO_2 back into the air. As a result of losing much of its blanket of "greenhouse gases" (H_2O and CO_2), the earth would cool off, especially near the poles and on mountaintops.

Land cools much more quickly than water, so the earth would have cold continents and warm oceans for the first few hundred years after the Flood. Water evaporating from the warm oceans would fall as snow near the poles, building up the ice sheets and glaciers that, at a maximum, covered 30 percent of the continents. We're still in the so-called Ice Age, since 10 percent of the post-Flood continents are still covered in ice, but the ice began to retreat from its maximum coverage perhaps 4,000 years ago, about 500 years after the Flood.

The big difference between cold, dry continents and warm, moist oceans would also generate colossal thunderstorms and tornadoes after the Flood. Over the tropical oceans, "super hurricanes" or hypercanes would develop that were ten times more powerful than Hurricane Katrina that devastated the Gulf Coast in 2005. Hurricanes today produce a certain pattern of bumps in sand underwater (hummocky cross stratification, or HCS, a "bubble wrap" pattern). Geologists have discovered the same pattern in fossil deposits — except the bumps or hills are much larger, implying much larger hurricanes known as hypercanes.

The low-pressure eye (center) of a hurricane acts like a straw that "sucks up" a hill of water from beneath it. Much of a hurricane's worst damage is produced when this hill of water, part of the storm surge, crashes onto shore. Depending on the shape of the sea bottom, wind speed and direction, moon tides, and other factors, hurricanes today can produce a storm surge 10–40 feet (3–13 m) high! Hypercanes in the first few centuries following Noah's flood might have produced storm surges, like a super tsunami, over 100 feet (30 m) high and many miles (many km) wide!

Land in South Florida today hardly ever rises over 20 feet (6 m) above sea level. A huge hypercane could "suck up" whales, dolphins, sharks, and shells in a 100-foot (30 m) hill of water over 100 miles (160 km) wide, and that storm surge crashing ashore would bury these big sea creatures in a "hash" of sand and shells along with big land animals — just like we see in Florida's rivers, shell pits, and quarries today. So, we can extend the third biblical C, catastrophe, from the worldwide catastrophe of Noah's flood to the regional catastrophes of ice and storms in the first few centuries following (and indirectly produced by) the Flood. The Bible also states that great winds blew over the earth at the end of the Flood, and these may have produced huge dust storms and wind-blown (aeolian) deposits on a vast scale.

The most famous victims of the icy catastrophes and colossal storms

Mastodon skeleton

that followed Noah's flood are the mammoths and mastodons preserved by the thousands across Siberia and Alaska. Much of the world's ivory supply comes from their tusks. Some flesh is preserved, and there is talk of cloning mammoths by taking DNA or sperm from the few well-preserved frozen fossils and growing baby mammoths (or half-breeds) in elephant mothers. The most famous specimen is the Berosovka mammoth, found whole with stomach contents only partially digested and flowers that probably bloom in July still in its mouth. There are several theories about what catastrophe killed thousands of temperate zone creatures in summer — icy winds, floods of icy water, dust storms, and even ice from space. Evolutionists don't even try to explain how those fossil hordes could be frozen slowly and gradually over millions of years!

Cenozoic mammals probably include both those fossilized during the Flood (possibly parts of the Tertiary System GCD11) and those fossilized in post-Flood ice and storm catastrophes (especially the Quaternary, GCD12, including the so-called Ice Age).

Reminding us of the Cambrian explosion of life, mammals burst onto the fossil scene in astonishing complexity and variety at the base of the Tertiary paleosystem (GCD11). As soon as we find mammal fossils in abundance, we find kinds that fly, swim, run, climb, and burrow — with no hint that

Mammoth replica

any of these life forms evolved from or into any of the others. It's as if the rising Flood waters finally reached the upland environments where pre-Flood mammals and flowering plants lived.

Air-breathing marine mammals would also tend to be buried late in the Flood. The first fossilized bats are bats, whales are whales, dogs are dogs, squirrels are squirrels, and moles are moles. Thus, mammal fossils provide powerful evidence of creation.

Unfortunately, mammals also dramatically illustrate death (extinction) and decline in size and variety, the corruption of God's perfect creation that followed man's sin. One awesome mammal was the giant ground sloth that stood taller and weighed more than *T. rex*. It had claws up to 3 feet (nearly 1 m) long. That would scare off a grizzly bear, but coprolite evidence shows the sloth was just a vegetarian using its giant claws as a leaf rake. Fossil hunters working in the Peace River in Florida have found parts of these giant sloths. Frank Garcia, a family friend and outstanding amateur paleontologist, found a nearly complete skeleton of a giant ground sloth, including the huge claws, in a shell pit just east of Tampa Bay.

Even armadillos, found flattened on highways from Texas to Florida, once existed in giant forms, like the glyptodont, which was about the size of a Volkswagen car. Sections of their armor (scutes) sometimes look like thick fossil flowers, and they can be made into necklaces and bolo ties. Although mammals survived in the post-Flood world better than amphibians and reptiles, they still suffered decline. The saber-toothed cat, state fossil of both Florida and California, seems to be extinct, along with the two giants pictured on the previous page. Two varieties of elephant kind exist today, the big-eared African and little-eared Indian elephants, but there were once many more varieties: woolly mammoth, Columbian mammoth, mastodon, stegodon, and others.

Burial of fossil mammals certainly demonstrates the third biblical C, catastrophe. We already described both the super-storms (hypercanes) that may have produced Florida's fossil hash and the icy catastrophe that preserved Siberian and Alaskan mammoths. In addition, post-Flood mammals may have experienced another kind of catastrophe: over-hunting by people! Florida once teemed with elephants, sloths, llamas, camels, saber cats, rhinos, tapirs, and many other mammals. The state's Museum of Natural History tells us these creatures were hunted to extinction by the Native Americans, about 4,000 years ago (about 500–1,000 years after Noah's flood). Sometimes fossils are found with spear points and arrowheads embedded in the bones, and cuts and scrapes from knives and tools can be

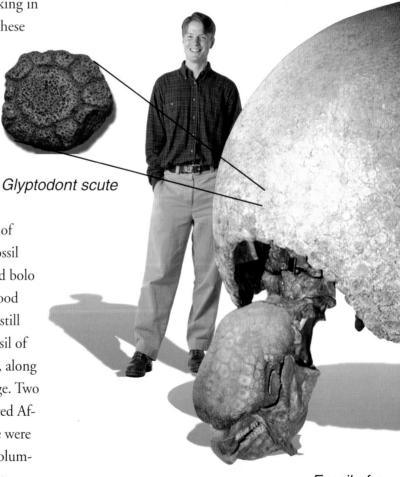

Glyptodont scute

Fossil of a glyptodont

seen. Cave paintings worldwide show man hunting mammoths. Just using spears, Pygmies in Africa still hunt elephants — and these are bigger animals than most dinosaurs!

Christ is the One who delivers from judgment and restores life. We see evidence of that in the way mammals that were spared on the ark multiplied and filled the earth. The generalized, adaptable bears God brought to Noah produced specialized, adapted black bears, grizzly bears, polar bears, and others as they multiplied to fill many different environments around the earth. Varieties of dogs, cats, and horses illustrate the tremendous variability God built into each of the created kinds!

Although creationists believe that fossil mammals demonstrate the effects of creation, corruption, catastrophe, and restoration, evolutionists attempt to support their view using fossils as well. Three kinds of mammals used as evolutionary examples are horses, whales, and the duck-billed platypus.

Hoof Dreams

A sequence of fossils that suggests how one kind of creature might have changed into others is called an evolutionary series. An evolutionary series consists of two parts: (1) a structural (morphologic) series that suggests how certain structures "morphed" (changed) into other structures, and (2) a fossil (stratigraphic) series that shows the differences in structure occurring in proper sequence from lower to higher in the GCD. At first glance, fossils of horses seem to be a perfect example of structural series + fossil series = evolutionary series!

The story begins with a fossil the size of a small dog that had four little hooves on its front feet and three little hooves on its hind feet. The animal had a short face with no gap (diastema) between the front and back teeth, and teeth suited for browsing (eating leaves and bark). Next come slightly larger animals

with three hooves on each foot. Then come larger animals still with three hooves per foot but a longer face and some gap between front and rear teeth. Finally we have large animals with one hoof per foot, a long face with a gap between the front and rear teeth, and teeth suited for grazing (eating grass). So, we have several structural or morphologic series: small to large size; many to one hoof per foot; short face to long face with a tooth gap; and grazing vs. browsing teeth.

What's more, these structural differences are found in stratigraphic series from lower to middle to upper Tertiary and into the present, with the whole evolutionary series presumed by evolutionists

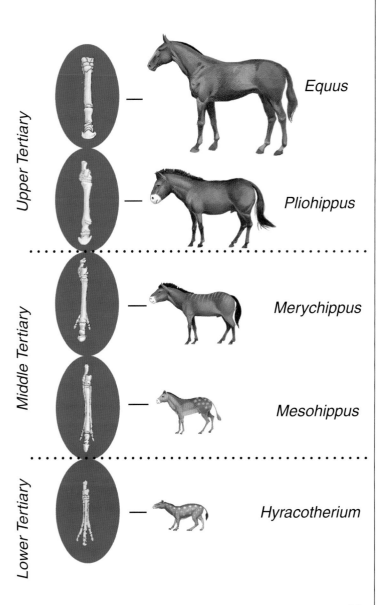

Equus

Pliohippus

Merychippus

Mesohippus

Hyracotherium

Upper Tertiary

Middle Tertiary

Lower Tertiary

to have taken over 60 million years. "Aha," says the evolutionist, "there's perfect fossil evidence for evolution. What's a creationist going to say about that?"

Creationists have many things to say. First of all, the animal at the bottom is not some mysterious pre-horse. It's a hyrax, what the Bible calls a rock badger or coney. They live in Africa and in zoos today. Evolutionists want to name the fossil "Eohippus," meaning "dawn horse," but the correct scientific name is *Hyracotherium,* which means "hyrax mammal." There are hyraxes today and there were hyraxes in the past; that sounds more like creation than evolution.

Miniature pony

Clydesdale

What about the size differences in the so-called horse series? Without any help from evolution, horse breeders have succeeded in just a few hundred years in producing horses as big as Clydesdales and as small as adults only 15 inches (38 cm) high! Have you always wanted a horse but live in an apartment or small house? If you can afford the price, there are now horses you could keep in your bedroom — and you could hold the "bales of hay" to feed them in the palm of one hand! The variation in size in the horse series is completely within the range of variation within kind.

Short face vs. long? Think about the differences between long-snouted collies and pug-nosed bulldogs. Again, the differences are no greater than variation within kind.

Many hooves vs. one hoof per foot? That's a little more interesting. Practically all land vertebrates (tetrapods, or four [tetra-] legged [-pod] creatures)

start off as embryos with a five-fingered (pentadactyl) plan. Then, like the variations on a theme used by creative artists, musicians, architects, and engineers, the five digits develop into an incredible number of different patterns. Modern one-toed horses actually keep parts of the two flanking toes as important leg support structures (not useless evolutionary leftovers) called splint bones. Occasionally, mistakes in development may produce a horse with two extra (and useless) side toes per foot. That doesn't make it less a horse, of course, just like cats and people born with a sixth finger (one of the more common, though still rare mistakes in development) are no less cats or people.

The difference between animals with three vs. one hoof per foot could be variation within kind, but the three-hoofed animals perhaps were a different created kind, now seemingly extinct. To be sure scientifically, we would have to conduct breeding experiments or do DNA tests, and that's not presently possible.

Evolutionists once believed and taught that whales evolved from cow-like animals; now they are touting wolf-like ancestors (mesonychids).

The three-hoofed animals would be better suited for walking on a "squishy" leaf-littered forest floor, and their teeth are like those of browsers that eat forest leaves and bark. The one-hoofed horses are better suited for running on prairies and they have teeth for grazing on grass, which is often much more gritty than leaves and bark. They seem designed for different environments.

Whether the three-hoofed and one-hoofed animals are the same created kind cannot be determined now, but it can be demonstrated that they are not parts of an evolutionary series. How? By stratigraphy — their position in the GCD. For example, in the John Day country of eastern Oregon, three- and one-hoofed fossils are found together. Think about this: volcanic ash could bury and fossilize animals around an African water hole; later, the skeletons of those fossils could be arranged in a morphologic series (sequence of sizes, shape, toe number, and similar characteristics). However, it would be known that one was not the ancestor of the other because all were living at the same time in the same place. The same is true of three- and one-hoofed fossils found together in Oregon.

Fossils of hoofed animals from South America make things even worse for evolution. There, large, one-hoofed animals are found lower in the geologic column

diagram than smaller, three-hoofed animals! It looks like hoof number may reflect ecology, instead of evolution. There were three-hoofed browsers living in forest environments at the same time there were one-hoofed grazers living in the grasslands. In North America, the forest environment with three-toed animals usually got buried in the rising Flood waters before or at the same time as the grassland environment with one-hoofed animals; in South America, the larger, one-hoofed grazers in the grassland environment got buried first.

To give evolutionists credit, the "horse story" as first told is what fossil evidence for an evolutionary series should look like — a graded series of differences in structure (morphologic series) spread from lower to higher in the geologic column diagram (stratigraphic series). It was only later fossil discoveries that forced the horse series, in the words of a famous evolutionist, to be "discarded or modified." Only a couple of other evolutionary series have even been proposed: the evolution from smooth to frilly suture lines in shelled squids (cephalopods), and the evolution from flat to coiled oysters. As discussed earlier, both these examples had to be "discarded or modified" as the result of fossil discoveries that supported creation and Flood geology much better than evolution.

Whale of a Tale

Today, stories of whale evolution are almost as popular — and just as unscientific — as stories of dinosaur-bird and horse evolution. Fossils of a greater variety of whales than we have living today are found, complete and complex, with the first abundant mammal fossils in lower Tertiary rock (GCD11). From rocks higher in the column (too late to be ancestral), some evolutionists are claiming to have put together a "walking whale," and they reinterpreted bones once thought to be those of a huge marine reptile to offer support for their view.

Several problems arise. Besides being too high stratigraphically, the bones were found jumbled together with those from many creatures, a condition allowing mistakes to be made very easily — such as putting the wrong head and body of a dinosaur together (the brontosaurus mistake), putting the head of a fish on the body of a bird (the hesperornis mistake), and a whole host of ape-man mistakes. Evolutionists claim bones in the pelvic region of modern whales are useless leftovers (vestiges) of rear legs in their ancestors; but far from being useless, these bones support organs necessary for whale reproduction!

Evolutionists contradict themselves on another point. Believing that evolution occurs as accidental mutations which produce forms that struggle to the death with each other, evolutionists teach that the first fish-amphibian links to flop out on land with all their genetic mistakes survived because there were no other land vertebrates to compete with them. That logic won't work the other way. Evolutionists aren't sure whether to say it was wolf-like or cow-like animals that evolved into whales, but the first to stick its mutated face under water to start evolving into a whale would get it pinched or bitten! Near-shore environments are incredibly rich in a whole array of fantastically well-adapted creatures and competition is intense. A half-adapted form wouldn't stand a chance. Not surprisingly, evolutionists have no theories about how whales (slowly, one genetic mistake at a time) evolved their ability to hold their breath so long and to dive to such great pressures. (You can imagine what would happen to the first half-whale that tried it!)

The Platypus: Reptile-Mammal Link?

Actually, most of the few fossils offered to support evolution are not a series at all, but just a single kind of creature claimed to have an unusual combination of traits. Remember the *Archaeopteryx* and coelacanth were once thought, respectively, to be reptile-bird and fish-amphibian links. Similarly, the duck-billed platypus *(Ornithorhynchus)* was once thought (and sometimes is still taught) to be a reptile-mammal link.

On our many trips to awesome Australia, we have had the pleasure of watching the playful platypus both in the wild and in zoos. The platypus looks like a beaver that crashed into a duck! It has webbed feet and a bill like a duck, but the bill is equipped with sensitive electrical detectors so that it can sense worms underwater where it hunts with its eyes shut. It's covered with hair (fur) and has a broad, flat tail like a beaver and is the size of a small beaver. It nourishes its young on milk, like all mammals do, but its young hatch from eggs that resemble those of reptiles. It's no wonder that, when the platypus was first reported to European scientists in 1795, some thought it was a fake stitched together by taxidermists (like the "jackalopes," jack rabbits with antlers, you can find in souvenir shops in the American West).

Some claimed the platypus was the survivor of a transitional form (missing link) that showed how egg-laying reptiles evolved into milk-giving mammals, but how did milk evolve? The evolutionist's answer: from sweat! Even when I believed in evolution, I had trouble with that one! Milk is a highly nutritious mixture of several different kinds of complex foods — proteins, fats, and sugars. Sweat is a waste product full of salts and various toxins (poisons). (It's no wonder that evolution needs so much time; think of all the little pre-platypus babies killed by drinking their mothers' sweat before a series of lucky accidents over millions of years turned sweat into good food!) Strike one.

The milk glands (the mammary glands for which mammals are named) supposedly evolved from sweat glands — but reptiles don't have sweat glands. Strike two.

Finally, fossils of the platypus and other monotreme mammals are found higher in the GCD than fossils of mammals that don't lay eggs — too late, therefore, to be their ancestors. Strike three.

Reflecting the familiar pattern, fossils of monotremes (egg-laying mammals) show a greater variety of forms and larger sizes than those still living today (a record of creation), followed by struggle and death and a decline in size and variety (corruption/catastrophe), with a remnant of these fascinating "missionary monotremes" preserved for us to enjoy today (restoration through Christ).

Duck-billed platypus (Ornithorhynchus)

CONCLUSION

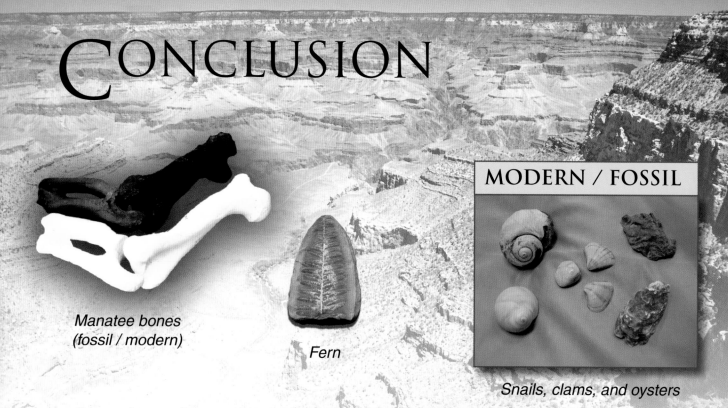

Manatee bones
(fossil / modern)

Fern

MODERN / FOSSIL

Snails, clams, and oysters

Comparing modern and fossil forms suggests living things began well designed to multiply after kind: CREATION.

Missionary Fossils

We've looked now at a lot of information about fossils. It seems Darwin was right about one thing: fossils are "the most obvious and serious objection to the theory" of evolution. Evolution is based on the fossils we do *not* find — the missing links that are still missing. The fossils we *do* find offer strong support for the four Cs of biblical history.

Creation

From blue-green algal stromatolites through trilobites and dinosaurs, to mammoths, the first buried fossils of each group are complete and complex, strong support for the biblical concept that each kind of life was created well designed to multiply after its own kind. Think about the Cambrian explosion; the first or lowest geologic system with abundant fossils includes the first fossilized clams, snails, nautiloids, horseshoe crabs, sea stars, fish, and more. Furthermore, the first fossilized member of each major group of animals is just as complete and complex as it is today, and with all the features that separate its kind from all the others.

As the rising waters of Noah's flood buried life zones with land plants and animals further up the geologic column diagram, it's the same story. The lowest land invertebrates preserved belong to complex and specialized groups. The first fossils of land vertebrates, the amphibians, are just as different from fish as salamanders are today. The first fossil birds were strong flyers with complex feathers. If we don't tell people that Christ is Creator, then as Jesus said, "The stones would cry out"! Design in fossils cries out in praise to the Creator!

Corruption

Unfortunately, fossils also illustrate the corruption of creation caused by mankind's sin. Fossils are dead things, and some fossils show evidence of disease and bite marks, suggesting that some animals were killed by others. Almost every group found as fossils shows evidence of decline in variety and size. There were once many more fantastic cephalopods, brachiopods, bryozoans, and crinoids, and much larger arthropods, reptiles, and mammals. When only a few members of once-great groups remain, they are called living fossils (e.g., chambered nautilus, sea lily). Some groups may be extinct, perhaps including the awesome trilobites and dinosaurs.

Based on "the war of nature, famine, and death" Darwin saw in our sin-cursed world, evolutionists believe that time, chance, struggle, and death (TCSD) have produced increasingly varied and complex life forms. Christians know, and scientists observe, that such presumed evolutionary processes make things worse, not better.

Catastrophe

Fossils are found as billions of dead things, buried in rock layers, laid down by water, all over the earth. All scientists agree that floods are the ideal conditions for forming fossils. When a plant or animal is rapidly and deeply buried in cement-rich sediment, the deep burial keeps the specimen from being totally destroyed by things like scavengers or wind and water currents, and the mineral cement hardens the material to preserve it.

Was it many small floods over millions of years that formed fossil deposits, or mostly the yearlong, worldwide flood of Noah's time? Several lines of scientific evidence, such as those below, suggest it was a lot of water, not a lot of time, which formed the fossil deposits.

1) Dead things are broken down so fast that most fossils must have formed rapidly or they wouldn't have formed at all.

2) Most fossils are found in sedimentary rocks that form in the way concrete cures, so the right conditions

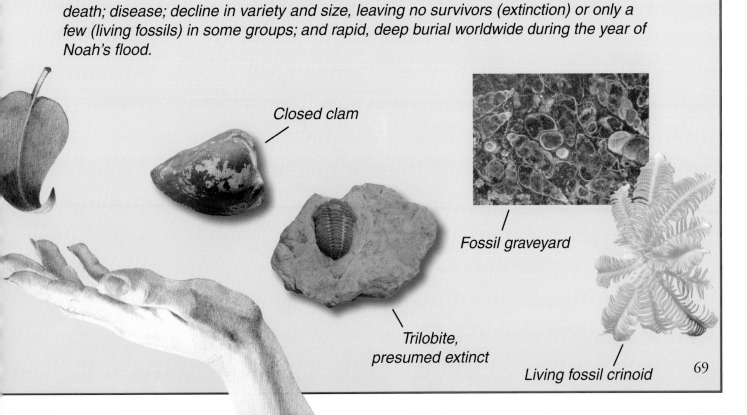

Because of mankind's sin, fossils also reflect CORRUPTION and CATASTROPHE: death; disease; decline in variety and size, leaving no survivors (extinction) or only a few (living fossils) in some groups; and rapid, deep burial worldwide during the year of Noah's flood.

Closed clam

Fossil graveyard

Trilobite, presumed extinct

Living fossil crinoid

Destruction left by Mount St. Helen's eruption

from various geologic systems lived at the same time in different places, not at different times in the same place. The systems in the geologic column seem to be primarily the buried remains of different life zones in the pre-Flood world.

7) Scientists studying the 1980 and 1982 eruptions of Mount St. Helens saw powerful evidence that catastrophic processes can do in days what slow processes could never do, not even in millions of years.

Even before science discovered the evidence to disprove evolution's myth of millions of years, we would have known from the gospel theme that fossils could not be millions of years old. Fossils tell us about struggle, disease, death, and disaster, but the Bible tells us that struggle, disease, death, and disaster were not part of the perfect world God created, but only entered after man's sin brought judgment into God's creation. Death and disaster could not be part of God's progressive process of creation millions of years before man's sin; otherwise Jesus would be opposing God's plan for creation when He came to put an end to struggle, disease, death, and disaster!

You may say (and some do) that man's sin only produced man's death — but the Bible says exactly the opposite. In Romans 8, Paul distinguishes between mankind, who sinned willfully, and the rest of creation, which was "subjected to futility not of its own will." Then Paul goes on to say that "the creation itself will be set free from its bondage to

form rock quickly and no amount of time can form rocks under the wrong conditions.

3) Some dinosaur bones and other fossils contain DNA, protein, or other chemicals that would break down completely in just thousands of years, not millions.

4) Countless numbers of living things must have been buried at the same time and place to form oil deposits, and that must have happened no more than thousands of years ago, or the oil would have leaked to the surface.

5) Gaps in the GCD with insufficient evidence of erosion, such as the "150 million missing years" in the walls of the Grand Canyon, suggest evolution's "millions of years" are a myth.

6) Misplaced fossils, like fossils of woody plants in Cambrian rock and living fossils, show that fossils

corruption and obtain the glorious liberty of the children of God." Because the whole universe was ruined by mankind's sin, salvation brings not only new life to human beings but also, when Christ returns in glory, "a new heaven and a new earth" (Rev. 21:1).

Remember, when science and Scripture seem to disagree, just wait; science (the study of God's world) will eventually catch up and find that God's Word has been right all along. You will be tempted, like Eve was, to put your own opinion and the words of "experts" above God's Word. You will be tempted, even by some Christians, to claim that your fossils are millions of years old. You will be tempted yourself to claim they are millions of years old, either to gain "intellectual approval," or just to hear the "oohs and aaahs" of the people to whom you're showing them. Let me encourage you instead to seek God's approval and to listen for the cries of "please tell me more" which will arise when you share your fossils the best way. This best way is not to tell about millions of years of struggle and death, but to tell about millions of miracles of creation, ruined by man's sin and the Flood, but restored to new life in Christ. The millions of years are not in the past out of reach to us; they are in the future for all who accept the free gift of salvation through Jesus Christ!

Christ

Evidence of awesome catastrophe and judgment blankets the earth, but the evidence of God's mercy is even greater. Even though we turned away from God, He did not turn away from us. Instead, He sent His own Son, Jesus Christ, who came willingly to pay the penalty for our sin (disobedience and rebellion) and to raise us to new life.

The evidence of God's mercy, healing, and restoration is everywhere. Spores and seeds sprouted in the "Flood mud" to once again cover the earth with food and beauty. The animals getting off the ark multiplied and filled the new environments all over the earth. Corals built those fantastic reefs again, providing homes for so many colorful sea creatures. The final restoration awaits the second coming of Christ, which will usher in the "new heavens and new earth." Then there will be no more death or tears; instead peace and harmony will be fully restored, with life, rich and abundant and forevermore.

All fossils echo the gospel theme: God's perfect creation, ruined by man, destroyed by the Flood, and restored to new life.

1) By their beauty, complex designs, and evidence of multiplication after kind, fossils point back to God's creation.

2) By their death, disease, and decline in size and variety, fossils tell us how man's sin brought corruption.

3) By their rapid burial in rock layers so deep and wide that they blanket the earth, fossils testify to worldwide catastrophe.

4) The preservation of living fossils and the multiplication of groups over the earth once again point toward the final restoration and new life in Christ.

As God saved the first world from the flood by Noah's ark, so God saves us from sin and death through new and eternal life in His Son, Jesus Christ.

APPLICATION:
HOW TO BUILD YOUR OWN
FOSSIL COLLECTION

Where Can I Find Fossils?

Fossils are not usually found in igneous and metamorphic rocks that have been very hot, like granite and lava flows. Most places, probably including the place where you live, have fossil–bearing sedimentary rocks such as limestones, sandstones, and shales. These rock layers, however, may be covered by soil or plants, so you need a place where the rock layers are easy to reach. Using words that start with the same sounds, the four major places to find fossils are cliffs, cuts, creeks, and quarries.

If there are no natural cliffs near you, there are usually artificial cliffs in road cuts and quarries, and at least shallow cliffs along a creek bank. The sedimentary rocks you are looking for are usually found in layers. The shale forms thin, flaky layers. Limestone is often white or grey and feels or marks like

chalk. Sandstone usually feels like sandpaper. Many cliffs have two or all three of these types of layers.

Road cuts have been a great blessing for fossil finders. Many states actually publish excellent guidebooks with detailed directions to specific fossil locations. A college, state university, or state geological survey may have such a book; ask your local librarian for help, or try online. Such books often have picture identification keys, too. Our family (that's two rock hounds and four pebble pups) used state guidebooks to find lots of fossils! Just be sure you find a safe place to park and to hunt, not in danger of traffic.

What Permission or Permits Do I Need?

Hunting fossils along public road cuts usually requires no special permission, except that some states require you to have a permit and/or to report any unusual specimens, especially vertebrate fossils.

Hunting in national parks or public preserves is usually forbidden or requires a special research permit. (I've been part of research teams with permits for work in the Grand Canyon, for example, but I cannot collect [except photographs] when I'm just hiking the canyon.) However, many rivers, beaches, deserts, and various wilderness areas often do have public access areas for fossil collecting. Fossil collecting trips in permitted areas can range from a canoe trip down south Florida's Peace River to a shark teeth fossil hunt on a southwest Florida beach. Hunters can join fossil searches in the California deserts; along lakeshores in Texas; and beside creeks in Ohio, Iowa, Nebraska, and other states. With permission, fossils can even be brought back from foreign countries such as Australia, New Zealand, Canada, Sweden, and Japan.

Hunting on private property requires permission of the landowner — and you need to tell the owner when, where, and for how long you would like to collect. Except in some foreign countries, fossil ownership usually belongs to the landowner. The owner often will let you collect many things for free, but you may have to work out a contract with the owner if you're going for, say, spectacular dinosaur or mammoth specimens! (We are helping to excavate a mammoth site in the Peace River Campground near our home in Arcadia, Florida, and the campground owner gave care of the fossils to a creationist group.) Some areas in America and Australia are so rich with fossils that owners simply charge a fee for hunting there, and let you keep what you find.

Quarries are great fossil sites. These include gravel pits, stone quarries, mine tailings

(leftovers), and shell pits mined for road fill in Florida. Some quarries offer supervised digs to school groups and other organized parties, but many have been closed by frivolous lawsuits and insurance costs. Exquisitely preserved seashells of many different kinds are found in shell pits near our Florida home, and sometimes fabulous vertebrates are found buried among them, including whales, mammoths, giant ground sloths, and even six-horned "giraffes." You need permission to hunt in abandoned quarries, and you need care to avoid quicksand, rock falls, deep water, and dangerous wildlife (such as alligators and snakes).

What Tools and Techniques Do I Need?

Hopefully, you will always need containers to hold your fossils: boxes, buckets, or bags. To protect small, delicate specimens, take along some tissue or cloth and some small, sealable containers, film bottles, or plastic bags. Always take a notepad or cards, camera, and a pencil or

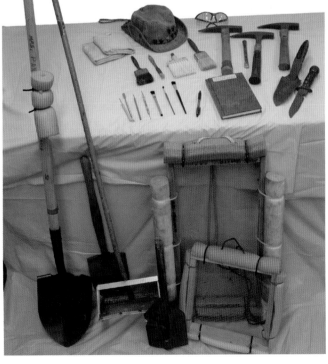

Common tools for fossil hunting

73

waterproof pen to record the place and time your fossils were found.

The excavating tools you need depend on the kinds of fossils you're hunting and the kind of material in which they're found. For example, if a group decides to hunt fossils which were buried in sand — either beach sand or the sand from the bottom or banks of a river like the Peace River in Florida — they will need specific tools. The basic tools needed to sieve through sand for fossils are a screen and a shovel or scoop to fill up the screen. Shaking a screen full of sand around in the water lets the sand fall through and leaves fossils and gravel behind. You can separate the fossils from the gravel by hand. Huge shark teeth, other fossil teeth, and big and small pieces of vertebrate bone, whole or in part, can be found in this way. Once in a great while, your shovel may even uncover a huge bone, like a mammoth tusk, too big for your screen!

The techniques for wet screening used in Florida can also be used for dry screening in drier environments, like East Africa where bones of apes and people (but not ape-men) have been found. A series of finer and finer screens can be used to look for microfossils.

Sometimes a big bone may be fragile or crumbly and need the protection of a plaster jacket for collection and transportation, as shown at right. Clean carefully around the fossil, leaving it attached to the surrounding material (matrix) only along a pedestal at the bottom.

Cover the fossil with a layer of dampened paper (e.g., toilet paper or "paleo-paper") or with aluminum foil. Sometimes sheets of foil molded around the fossil make a sufficient jacket without plaster.

Apply moist strips of plaster-soaked cloth around the fossil, rubbing each layer of plaster until it's smooth, molding it to the shape of the fossil. Let the first and last plaster strip go under the edge of the fossil to the matrix pedestal. The easiest form of plaster to use is the plaster gauze rolls doctors once used as wraps for broken bones. Strips can also be made, using light or heavy cloth (such as burlap) soaked in plaster-of-Paris added to a bucket of water according to directions on the box. Burlap strips cut 4 inches by 4 feet (10 cm by 1.25m) are easy to use on big specimens.

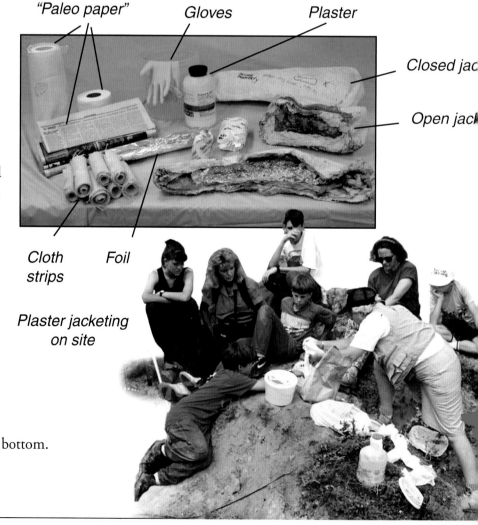

"Paleo paper" Gloves Plaster

Closed jacket

Open jacket

Cloth strips Foil

Plaster jacketing on site

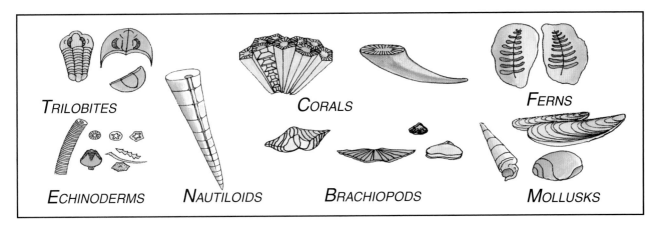

Major Invertebrate Groups and Ferns

For really big specimens, sticks or branches can be plastered into the jacket as splints for extra support in transport.

Let the jacket dry for perhaps an hour or two, depending on weather and size, less for small specimens.

When the jacket is dry, label it with a waterproof marker, indicating (directly or in code) the finder, place and time of discovery, type of fossil and its orientation in the jacket.

When the jacket is hard, loosen the base or pedestal by undercutting with a knife or chisel and hammer, depending on matrix strength. Then roll the jacket over quickly, taking it off its pedestal by applying pressure evenly along the fossil's length.

Transport your "open jacket" back to the lab (or your garage or bedroom), where the specimen can be unwrapped and studied without fear of losing or disorienting its parts. Sealing the opening with more plaster turns it into a "closed jacket."

Plaster jackets can be formed around specimens found in either sand or hard rock, but extracting fossils from rock is more difficult. A geological hammer is great for chipping fossils out of rock, but PROTECT YOUR EYES FROM ROCK CHIPS — WEAR GOGGLES! In general, don't chip too close to the specimen (unless it's loose), and angle your chipping away from the fossil. A hammer and a metal chisel can be used in place of a geological hammer, and a pickax (exercise care when using this) may be helpful in breaking off big pieces of rock. Back home, you may want to use brushes and dental tools to clean rock matrix sticking to your fossils.

How Do I Recognize and Name My Fossils?

The good news is that most fossils are easy to identify because things living today and fossils are both descendants of the same created kinds. Fossil clams look like clams, snails like snails, corals like corals, ants like ants, sharks like sharks, turtles like turtles, elephants like elephants, and so on. Only a few major groups, perhaps dinosaurs and trilobites, may have become completely extinct, and the features in these creatures are still very similar to those living today.

We hope, of course, that the pictures in this book will be a big help. Invertebrates, especially seashells, are the most common fossils by far, and also the easiest to identify, because they are often found complete or nearly so. Major invertebrate groups and their key features are reviewed above. Learn to recognize these, and you'll be able to recognize the major groups to which most of your fossils belong. Then you can use state guidebooks and other fossil guidebooks with pictures to identify your fossils

SWIRL AND SHAPE VARIATION IN TEETH

1) Rhinoceros
2) Mammoth (baby tooth)
3) Mastodon
4) Beaver
5) Horse, upper
6) Camel
7) Cave bear
8) Bison
9) Horse, lower
10) Small bear
11) Tapir jaw
12) Alligator
13) Manatee
14) Whale

Perhaps hardest to identify are fragmentary pieces of vertebrate bone. It helps to be familiar with the general shapes of leg bones, back bones, ribs, shoulder blades, pelvis, jaw, etc. Finding joint surfaces is a big help, too.

more specifically. Never mind the big names; most fossil identifications are done by matching your specimen to pictures (and be sure to note the size scale). Unfortunately, many guidebooks will "preach" evolution and millions of years, but the fossil identifications are still good. With practice, you'll be able to identify many fossils by sight.

Many plant parts are clear and complete enough to identify easily from picture guidebooks. Because of their hard outer coating, teeth are often very well preserved. However, there are so many subtle variations in shapes and in patterns of markings on the cutting surfaces of teeth that a lot of care and close examination may be needed for proper identification.

Perhaps the best thing is to ask an expert, or someone with local fossil experience. Many areas have fossil clubs, workshops, gem and mineral shows, museums, and colleges with geology or paleontology departments. You may have to listen to beliefs about evolution and millions of years, but you may also get your fossil identified and learn how to do it yourself. You may even be able to share what you've learned about creation, the Fall, the Flood, and salvation. We belong to a fossil club that includes both creationists and evolutionists, and we're free to share our ideas as we all share our enthusiasm for fossils.

How Do I Store My Fossils?

Most shells, teeth, and heavily mineralized specimens need no special care beyond cleaning, although a little acrylic spray may help them shine. Lightweight, spongy, or crumbly bones need to be sealed and hardened. Let the specimen dry slowly (days or weeks), progressively cleaning it gently as it dries. Then immerse the fossil in a concrete sealer, providing plenty of time for air bubbles to escape and for the sealer to penetrate deeply. To take it out, support the fossil as you raise it from the sealer. A screen is good for this. (Save the sealer to use again.) As the fossil dries, the cloudy blue covering will turn clear.

How Do I Display My Fossils?

You can display your fossils by group, type, locality, etc. You can also use your fossils to help spread the gospel message by arranging them in a manner that demonstrates the four Cs of biblical history:

1) Under creation you could put fossils that show complex beginnings, like trilobites and nautiloids, or specimens comparing modern organisms and fossils, like clams, snails, crabs, fern leaves, or ants to show multiplication after kind.

2) To illustrate corruption you can display fossils showing disease or bite marks. Any fossil can be used to demonstrate death, and some, like dinosaur bones or trilobites, illustrate probable extinction. A tooth display could be used to show how sharp, pointed teeth and bird bills can be used to eat either plants (creation) or meat (corruption).

3) Many things about fossils point back to the catastrophe of Noah's flood and the Ice Age that followed: (a) fossil graveyards — rock slabs with jumbles of organisms all buried together; (b) closed clams buried so deep and fast they couldn't open their shells and burrow out; (c) samples of coal and oil formed from the crushed remains of plants and animals; (d) crinoids, cephalopods, brachiopods, and bryozoans all demonstrate decline in size and variety.

4) To point toward the mercy and restoration of all things in Christ, you could display the preservation (salvation) of living fossils; show the beauty of form and color among forms that got off the ark to multiply and re-fill the earth; and use Christ's words to compare the judgment by water in the past (the Flood) with the judgment by fire in the future. Always remember, and share with others, the "good news" that the final judgment is followed by the glory of new life in the new heavens and new earth (2 Pet. 3). "Even so, come Lord Jesus" (Rev. 22:20).

1) Creation
The nautilus shows God created living things well designed to multiply after kind.

2) Corruption
Man's sin brought death, disease, and decline, perhaps even extinction to trilobites and dinosaurs.

3) Catastrophe
Fossil "graveyards" and closed clams worldwide suggest rapid deep burial during Noah's flood.

4) Christ
Sin brought death, but God saved "living fossils" from the Flood, and Jesus saves forever all who believe.

Bibliography

Austin, Steven A., (ed.). *Grand Canyon: Monument to Catastrophe.* Santee, CA: ICR, 1994.

Bliss, Richard B., Gary E. Parker, and Duane T. Gish. *Fossils: Key to the Present.* Santee, CA: ICR, 1980.

De Young, Don. *Thousands . . . Not Billlions.* Green Forest, AR: Master Books, 2005.

Gish, Duane T. *Evolution: the Fossils Still Say No!* Green Forest, AR: Master Books, 1995.

Morris, Henry M., and Gary E. Parker. *What is Creation Science?* Green Forest, AR: Master Books, 1994.

Parker, Gary E. *Creation: Facts of Life.* Green Forest, AR: Master Books, revised edition, 2006.

Parker, Gary E., and Mary M. Parker. *Skeletons in Your Closet.* Green Forest, AR: Master Books, 1982.

Parker, Gary E., and Mary M. Parker. *Dry Bones . . . and Other Fossils.* Green Forest, AR: Master Books, 1979, 1995.

Vail, Tom, (ed.). *Grand Canyon: A Different View.* Green Forest, AR: Master Books, 2003.

Illustration / Photo Credits

Photos of fossil hunting scenes and equipment supplied by **Dr. and Mrs. Parker.**

Fossils supplied by Dr. and Mrs. Parker from the **Creation Adventures Museum** in Arcadia, Florida, were photographed by **David Lombardi** and **Cornelia Bularca.**

Corbis — 4T, 34, 42T, 52T

Getty — 39B

Science Photo library — 46, 48T, 49, 57B, 58B

Photos.com — 6T, 18T 22T, 22B, 24, 26T, 33B, 35B, 36B, 38B 40T, 44, 48B, 57T, 72T

Super Stock — 37

Jamie Brandt — 5, 25, 52M, 64, 65

Dr. and Mrs. Parker — 6, 7, 8, 9, 10, 11, 12, 13, 15, 17TB, 19, 23, 26B, 27T, 34, 35T, 28B, 32, 36T, 37B, 38T, 39T, 41, 42B, 43, 45, 46B, 47, 50, 51TB, 53, 54B, 58T, 59, 62, 68T, 69B, 72T, 73, 74, 75,76, 77

Bryan Miller — 8M, 17M, 20, 21, 27B, 33T, 54T, 55, 63, 67

Tom Vail (Canyon Ministries) — 28T, 30, 31

Bill Looney — 29B, 70, 71

Darrel Wiskur — 51T

NASA — 60

Glossary

4 Cs — an aid for remembering four major events in biblical history important to understanding fossils: God's perfect Creation, ruined by man's sin (Corruption), destroyed by Noah's flood (Catastrophe), restored to new life in Christ.

Cambrian explosion — the sudden appearance of a wide variety of complex life forms in the lowest rock layer with abundant fossils (Cambrian); considered a challenge to evolution, these may be the first organisms in a corrupted creation to be buried in Noah's flood.

creationist — one who thinks that (1) fossils show complex and separate beginnings because each kind was created well designed to multiply after kind, but that (2) fossils also show death, disease, and decline in variety and size because struggle and death followed man's sin (until Christ returns) and brought on Noah's flood.

evolutionist — one who believes fossils will show that (1) millions of years of time, chance, struggle, and death changed a few simple life forms into all the complex and varied forms we have today, and that (2) new structures gradually developing from low to high in the geologic column will be seen when "missing links" are eventually found.

fossil — remains or traces of a once-living thing preserved by natural processes, most often by rapid, deep burial in water-laid sediments.

geologic column diagram (GCD) — twelve major groups of fossils (see geological system) diagrammed in a vertical series intended to show either (a) stages in evolution over millions of years, or (b) stages in the burial of different environmental zones mostly during the year of Noah's flood.

geologic system — a major rock layer whose fossils are used to name it for one of the 12 groups in the geologic column diagram.

index fossils — fossils used to identify a geologic system (see above) because they lived either (a) at a certain time or (b) in a certain place in the pre-Flood world.

paleontology — the study of fossils.

paraconformity — a gap without erosion in the geologic column diagram; breaks the time sequence assumed by evolution, and may suggest fossils from different environments were rapidly buried by a lot of water, not a lot of time.

permineralized — fossils preserved by minerals hardening in the pore spaces of a specimen such as a shell, bone, or wood.

petrified — fossils preserved by minerals completely replacing but preserving the pattern in the original wood, bone, etc.

polystrates — fossils that cut through many layers, suggesting the sequence was laid down very rapidly.

sediments — particles of sand, silt, clay, ash, etc. eroded and deposited by wind and water currents; most fossils are found in sedimentary rocks which form, like concrete does, when sediments are mixed in the right amounts with water and rock cement minerals such as lime ($CaCO_3$) and silica (SiO_2).

stratigraphic series — sequence of fossils from lower to higher in the geologic column diagram (see above); thought to represent either (a) stages in evolution or (b) stages in burial during Noah's flood.

Index

Coming Spring 2007...

creationmuseum

www.AnswersinGenesis.org